THE BURNING BUSH

"Whenever the interior flame is lacking, there have to be commandments written on tables of stone . . . If today we abstain from killing, lying, stealing, committing adultery, it is no longer because these things have been the subject of prohibitions written on tables of stone, but because someone has lived in a certain way and has died in a certain way."

God revealed himself to Moses on Mount Horeb as a fire which burns but does not consume. Jesus, Lev Gillet tells us, is the fullest manifestation of the God who revealed himself to Moses in the burning bush. He is the one who shows us how to undertake the way he lived, a way which reveals "the God of Limitless Love," the love which burns but does not consume.

Then Gillet turns to what is perhaps the most popular of all psalms, psalm 23 — the "shepherd psalm". He discloses the deepest meanings of this psalm, showing us the familiar words in a way we have never seen them before. The shepherd psalm is a mirror in which we see reflected the whole of the Christian life, and the attitude which we ought to bring to God and to our prayer.

Lev Gillet is a monk of the Orthodox Church. He is presently serving as chaplain to the Fellowship of St. Alban and St. Sergius, an organization dedicated to furthering mutual understanding and co-operation between the divided Christians of East and West.

THE BURNING BUSH

BY

ARCHIMANDRITE LEV GILLET

Prepared for publication
by Constance Babington Smith

TEMPLEGATE PUBLISHERS
SPRINGFIELD, ILLINOIS 62705

© 1976 by
The Fellowship of St. Alban and St. Sergius
St. Basil's House
1 Canterbury Road
Oxford OX2 6LU
England

Published in the United States of America by
Templegate Publishers
302 East Adams Street
Post Office Box 5152
Springfield, Illinois 62705-5152
217-522-3353
templegate.com

ISBN 0-87243-063-4

The author gratefully acknowledges the assistance of Miss Constance
Babington Smith in preparing this book for publication.

CONTENTS

I

THIS GREAT SIGHT

*And Moses said, I will now turn aside,
and see this great sight, why the bush
is not burnt. (Ex. 3:3)*

The great vision granted to Moses was one of the main
turning points in the history of the Jewish people. The incident is known as the Burning Bush, in both the Jewish and
the Christian traditions. And I would like to give the same
title to the addresses in this retreat because, if you agree, our
subject is going to be the Burning Bush itself, along with its
spiritual implications.

First of all let us picture the episode in its biblical context.
Moses, in the Egyptian desert, was looking after the flocks of
his father-in-law Jethro. Wending his way across the desert
he came to Horeb, 'the mountain of God'. And it was there
that the angel of the Lord, or rather the Lord God himself in
the shape of an angel, appeared to him in the midst of
flames of fire. The flames were blazing out of a bush. Yet
the bush was not consumed or destroyed. Moses was overcome with amazement. He decided to turn aside, to deviate
from his intended course, so as to gain a closer view of 'this
great sight' and to see 'why the bush is not burnt'.

Let us pause here a moment to consider two points. Firstly,
where did the incident of the Burning Bush take place? On
the mountain called Horeb. Geographically this mountain
may be regarded as part of Sinai. But historically and
spiritually Horeb and Sinai have utterly different connota-
tions. One is the mountain where Moses saw the Burning

Bush, the other the mountain where he received the divine Commandments—the Tables of the Law. If the Jewish people had been able to live according to the vision of the Burning Bush, they would not have needed the Tables of the Law. But for those who remained untouched by the revelation of Horeb the revelation of Sinai was necessary. Whenever the interior flame is lacking, there have to be commandments written on tables of stone. This truth is just as valid for us now as for the Jews of the Old Testament.

The second point concerns Moses's turning aside from his original path. He felt that the marvel of the Burning Bush warranted making a stop; he was moved with desire to contemplate it and ponder deeply on it. He accepted without question this sudden, extraordinary, divine event. And it was because he did not hesitate to change his direction towards the Burning Bush that God was able to call to him. 'And when the Lord saw that . . . [Moses] turned aside to see, God called unto him out of the midst of the bush, and said, Moses, Moses. And he said, Here am I.' [1]

All this applies just as much to us today as it did to Moses. If during the course of our lives we hurry along without stopping, without even a glance towards the Burning Bush (which nevertheless continues its blazing along the whole of our way, though most of the time our eyes are closed to it), we shall miss the opportunity God desires. If, on the contrary, we do not hesitate to leave aside for a time the flocks of Jethro—our daily cares—the Lord will call to us from the midst of the bush. He will call to each one of us by a name that is our own.

Moses answered 'Here am I' without knowing what God would require of him. Such a declaration of being at his disposal is what the Lord awaits from us also. So, as this retreat

[1] Ex. 3 : 4.

is beginning, may we place ourselves before him, before the Burning Bush, saying: 'Here am I. Here am I at this very moment. Here am I in this very place. Here am I for Thee, without any reservations whatever.'

Now let us return to the biblical narrative. We might perhaps have expected that God would have encouraged Moses to come running towards him at once. But not at all. 'And . . . [the Lord] said, Draw not nigh hither: put off thy shoes from off thy feet, for the place whereon thou standest is holy ground.' [2]

For us, likewise, an approach to the Burning Bush is not such an easy matter as might be imagined. First there is the ascent of Mount Horeb (most of the divine visions in the Old Testament took place on mountains). In order to draw near to God we must begin by climbing up above the plain, by disengaging ourselves from its worries, thus gradually attaining to altitudes where the perspectives are longer and the air purer. This climb is not without difficulties. There are the hazards of the way. There is also the burden of one's own body, the effort of disciplining the flesh, which is so often unwilling (the eternal opposition between gravity and grace). But the upward climb is not all. We must furthermore bare our feet, we must take off our shoes. We cannot, we must not, desecrate the holy ground of God's presence with any mud or even dust that may have accumulated on our feet during the journey.

'The place whereon thou standest is holy ground.' This saying belongs essentially to the Old Testament. Since the time when it was spoken—ever since we have learnt that we are no longer under the law but under grace—a new light has illumined the entire scene. There have always been certain

[2] Ex. 3 : 5.

9

places which by virtue of their history or by a special act of consecration have been set apart. But we know now that every place where we meet the Lord can become a holy place. The road we follow, the street we cross, the train, the factory, the field, the room, the hospital, the school; all these places can become 'temples' for us, where we worship God in spirit and in truth, sanctuaries where God calls to us by our own names. The Burning Bush is to be found everywhere.

So here we are, at this very moment, before the Burning Bush, before 'this great sight'. The time has come to ask ourselves what the vision means and 'why the bush is not burnt'. Like every other episode in the history of salvation, the Burning Bush has several meanings. Among these some are secondary but one remains essential.

First let us glance at the immediate historical significance of the Burning Bush. It was needful for Moses to become aware of his vocation. The children of Israel were being oppressed in Egypt. God had taken pity on his people. Thus he said to Moses: 'I have surely seen the affliction of my people . . . and heard their cry. . . . I know their sorrows; and I am come down to deliver them . . . and this shall be a token unto thee, that I have sent thee.'[3] The bush in flames thus represented to Moses the sufferings of Israel under foreign oppression. And the fact that the bush, although on fire and burning, was not destroyed, expressed the divine protection and formed a symbol, a pledge, of hope and liberation.

Although this aspect of the Burning Bush is a secondary one it is, from the historical viewpoint, the most directly relevant. Yet it has a universal meaning which still applies to us today. In times of suffering we may, like Israel in Egypt,

[3] Ex. 3 : 7, 8, 12.

feel ourselves maimed and burnt. But the spiritual vision of the Burning Bush assures us that the flames will not devour or destroy us. A Supreme Compassion strives for us in the midst of the holocaust, takes our part against it, so that we shall not be consumed or annihilated. 'I have seen the affliction . . . I am come down to deliver.'

Now let us consider another secondary meaning of the Burning Bush. What was it exactly that was being burnt? Not a fine tree, thick with foliage and fruit. Not a beautiful plant covered with flowers, fragrant with scent. It was a bush, in other words a wild plant lacking in any beauty, a small clump of brushwood, a stunted shrub, untidy, unproductive, with thorns that prick and gash and tear. For such plants as this the term 'weeds' comes at once to mind.

In the burning up of weeds (which nevertheless are not consumed) there is also a universal and present meaning. Noxious weeds represent the soul abandoned to sin. The divine fire purifies without destroying. It is imperative to throw into this fire our dead wood, our thorns, our weeds. The Burning Bush is a symbol of purification.

We have now considered two aspects of the Burning Bush, both of them secondary though nonetheless of universal importance. But we have not yet touched upon the essential and eternal significance of the 'great sight'. The Burning Bush has a meaning far surpassing that of divine protection against the flames of suffering, far surpassing the divine purification which is at the same time painful and liberating. This supreme meaning is beyond and above both of these others. The time has now come to yield ourselves to what this signifies, to this ultimate revelation.

Here is the deepest meaning of the Burning Bush: it is

the visible expression of the very nature of God. The Burning Bush symbolises the divine essence. This claim demands further explanation. In the vision of the Burning Bush there are two elements. Firstly there is a fire, there are flames. Then there is a bush which is burnt by the fire and yet remains unharmed. The fire of the Burning Bush is, obviously, God himself. God is a devouring fire. But what kind of fire? A fire of anger, of punishment, of destruction, vengeance? Certain passages in the Bible seem to tend towards this interpretation, but they are anthropomorphisms; they are human —excessively human—figures of speech. The whole of the great spiritual tradition of Christianity—that of the New Testament, of the Fathers of the Church, of the saints—sees in this divine fire, in the fire of the Burning Bush, in the fire which seems to have a passion for self-communication, the incandescent charity of the Lord, the incandescence indeed of his love.

His love. . . . Not without some hesitation do I dare to make use of that word. It has so often been abused, so often profaned! Yet we must not forget that the one and only definition of God in the New Testament is in the words 'God is love'.[4]

God is fire. God is love. God is a self-propagating emotional power, a fire that shares itself. Centuries after Moses beheld the flames of the Burning Bush, this same fire merged with the tongues of flame at Pentecost, and with the fire that burned within the hearts of the disciples at Emmaus.

In saying that God is a fire of love we are certainly stating a truth that plays havoc with many of our ideas, in fact almost all our ideas. But we must be more precise. Since we are meditating on the Burning Bush we must be quite clear as to how the vision of the bush of Horeb differs from the

[4] I John 4 : 16.

many other concepts of God which also speak of God as fire and love. What is there that is so special about 'this great sight'? What does the vision of Moses insist on? This we shall try to discover in our next meditation. For the moment let it suffice to have established the following fundamentals: God is a fire of love, burning the bush without destroying it; God can set fire to me also without destroying me. We have said with Moses: 'I will turn aside and see this great sight, why the bush is not burnt'. But it is not enough to contemplate from outside. God calls to me and speaks to me from the very heart of the bush. O Lord, prepare me to enter into the Burning Bush itself!

II

LIMITLESS LOVE

*And Moses said unto God: Behold, when
I come unto the children of Israel and
shall say unto them: The God of your
fathers hath sent me unto you; and they
shall say to me: What is his name?
what shall I say unto them? (Ex. 3:13)*

We have already seen, in our first meditation, that the
Burning Bush is more than a symbol of the divine protection
granted to a soul burdened by temptations, more than the
purifying of a soul disfigured by stains. The Fire that burns
without spending itself, and without destroying, expresses
the very essence of God—incandescent love. We must now
discover how it is that this vision of divine love, unlike the
many other renderings of the same love, has a unique
meaning.

Like Moses, we are here before the Bush. Like Moses we
are saying to God 'Tell me thy name. Under what name shall
I proclaim thee to men?'. What then is the divine name that
the vision of Horeb brings to us? We know what great
importance was attached in ancient times (both pagan and
biblical) to the knowledge of divine names. To know the
name of a divinity was in some degree to possess him, to
participate in his being and power. The practice of the 'Jesus
prayer' (the continuous invocation of the name of Jesus) in
the Orthodox Church, the Moslem technique of *dhikr*, or
repetition of the divine attributes, the term 'Master of the
Name', *baal shem,* accorded in the Jewish tradition to certain

saints or mystics—all of these testify to the enduring vitality of the spiritual paths centring upon the name of the Lord. God has many names. He has as many names as there are moments when he reveals himself to us. He is always the same and yet always different.

But we ourselves are often wearing a mask, we assume a disguise, when we pretend that we are adoring God. We approach him not as we really are but as we want others to see us, as we want God himself to see us. Such a situation is not genuine, it is not true. Furthermore we often worship God under a name which is not his. Here too genuineness is lacking. We should ask ourselves, each time we approach God, each time we speak to him, what aspect of himself he is revealing to us at this moment. Then we must address ourselves to him under that special aspect, under that special name.

Nowadays in the context of 'controversial' theology or philosophy there is much talk of 'the death of God'. This expression is obviously absurd. God does not die. But there is a certain concept of God which dies (and we ought to rejoice that this is so) namely the concept of a distant God, metaphorically seated on a heavenly throne, distributing blessings and punishments to his creatures. A transcendent sovereign, accessible only with difficulty.

The God to whom we aspire, the God we can love, is the God who assuredly transcends us but is also our most intimate, most profound, interior reality—in short the God who is love. But is it under this name that we know him? Is it under this name that we worship him?

Questions of vocabulary are often extremely important. The word 'God' has become sacred by means of a very long tradition, by universal usage, and by liturgical use. This word, this name, is the heart and strength of innumerable souls. To disparage it would be blasphemous. There is no question of discarding it. Yet this does not prevent us from noticing two things. First of all the word 'God', from the etymological and linguistic point of view, lacks a definite and precise content. It possesses such breadth that it can sometimes seem empty. Furthermore it is possible to use this name in a routine or mechanical way, it can be treated as a meaningless formula. On the other hand at certain times, when a particular experience of God is granted to us, this name that is so all-embracing may seem to us inadequate to express strongly enough the divine aspect which, in that particular moment, in those actual circumstances, has revealed itself to us. Rather than saying 'God', or 'My God', or 'Thou who art God', or 'Lord God', we shall sometimes find a more real stimulus if we say 'Thou who art Beauty', 'Thou who art Truth', 'Thou who art my life', 'Thou who art my light', 'Lord who art my strength', 'Lord who art my forgiveness'—and so on. In certain circumstances, and to certain souls, I have advised this use of individual, concrete realities rather than of an abstract term. I think they have been helped by the substitution.

It would be dangerous to put metaphysical attributes in the place of the living and personal God, to dissolve the Person or rather the ultimate Supra-Person in psychological or moral entities. But we must never lose sight of the fact that we can adore the same unique and eternal Being under a thousand different names.

If we believe that God is Love, if we believe that the experience of God, in the shape of Love, constitutes the supreme reality, it will become natural to us to think of God, and to speak of him as 'Lord of Love' or simply as 'the Lord Love'. This may change our whole horizon. It is not a matter of deifying a subjective idea of love. It is a matter of reaching towards the Beloved, who is the source of *all* love.

Now let us return to the Burning Bush. 'Tell me thy name.' 'O Love, thou who wast long ago, in this moment of history, and who art now, in this instant of my personal life, explain thyself to me by means of this sign, reveal to me what is the true meaning of the vision of Horeb.'

To Moses's question the Lord now makes a reply: 'I am Yaveh'. But what is the relationship between this answer 'I am' and the Burning Bush? The exact meaning of the word 'Yaveh' has been, and still remains, the subject of different interpretations. 'I am Yaveh' can mean 'I am he who is', or 'I am what I am', or alternatively 'I am now the one who I shall be', or 'I am that which I wish to be'. But all these interpretations have a common basis. All relate to the idea of being, and of the Divine Being.

And since this definition of the being of God was given on Horeb, in the context of the Burning Bush, the biblical text establishes a certain relationship between the vision of the Bush and the revelation of the name of the Lord. A historian, a strict biblical scholar, might perhaps contest this interpretation. But I claim the right to maintain it on the spiritual plane. Thus the conjunction of the vision and the revelation of the divine name conveys the following message: 'You ask what my name is. I am Being. I am the Being whom you see in being at this very moment. Look before you. You see the Bush that burns without being consumed. You see fire. The Being I am is a Being of fire. These flames proclaim my love. But look more carefully. My fire does not destroy. That which it burns it purifies and transforms into itself, makes part of itself. And my flame has no need to be fed. It imparts itself, gives itself. I am the Gift that never ceases to give itself. I am that which you have seen me to be on Horeb. My being, my essence (in that I am Yaveh) merges with my love. But the love I now reveal to you, under the symbol of the Burning Bush, is my love insofar as it never ceases to love and to burn, insofar as no limits circumscribe it or stop it. Together the Burning Bush and the name of Yaveh signify my inexhaustible bounty. I am Limitless Love.'

Limitless Love. . . . These words which I have just spoken are what I want to make the very heart of this retreat. Of course we already know God as Love. But I would now like to consider with you more closely the special significance of 'God-Love' as Limitless Love.

The Love that gushes forth from God is limitless in time. It is eternal because the Lord Love is eternal. The Lord Love has always loved and will love for ever. He has loved, in his own heart, each being, of no matter what kind, animate or inanimate, even before it was created as an individual being (as distinct from the divine Being). What is creation? Every act of creation is an act of love. Creation is also the act whereby that which already, in God, was an interior object of love becomes henceforth an exteriorised object of love, receives existence from God, becomes capable of entering with God into the relationship that expresses itself by the pronouns 'I', 'thee', 'thou'.

This is my own story. This is your own story. The history of each one of us is a history of love. The Lord of Love has loved me, myself, from all eternity, first of all within himself, then through the millions of ancestors of whom I am the descendant. My present existence is the climax of an unfolding of love and grace. And if I glance back over the course of my own personal life, ever since my first memories, I see passing before me all thy goodness, Lord of Love, and

I recognise it now even where, at the time, it seemed that all lovingkindness was absent.

Love is limitless in space. Have you ever considered the 104th Psalm? In the Orthodox Church it is said every evening at the beginning of Vespers. Read it carefully. In it the whole universe passes by, the mountains and the sea, the wind and the storms, the wild beasts and the humblest little animals, the trees and the rocks. It is a whole cosmology, which ought to guide our piety towards avenues far wider than any 'private' relationship with God. What we need to do is to let ourselves be carried away by the immense current of Limitless Love, by that impulse, that progression of all nature which, according to Saint Paul, awaits liberation from the consequences of the Fall. Nevertheless we must beware lest the ascent of man towards God obscures for us the descent of God towards man.

Take a flower in your hand, take a stone. Ponder upon them, not from the scientific angle of the botanist or the geologist, but from the spiritual viewpoint. Each of them is an epitome of the evolution of the world towards the 'total Christ' of whom Saint Paul speaks. But they are not only signs of Love reaching towards the peaks. They are also signs of Love coming towards us, revealing itself to us, giving itself to us, coming ever closer and closer. Gaze on the divine beauty in a blade of grass, in a leaf, in a branch. Perceive an offering in a scent, in a colour. Let us integrate our spiritual lives with the life of the universe. Let us recognise in every creature a spring of divine love fitting to itself, and to itself alone. The Lord Love has loved each grain of sand, each stone, each leaf, each shrub, each animal.

To unite ourselves to all this, to enter into that great rising and falling tide of love, to adore God and to give thanks to him in the name of nature (which cannot speak)—this is cosmic piety'. This is our reply to Limitless Love.

Do you love the Sun? Do you love the stars? Do you love the galaxies? Do you thank God for their creation and for their presence? Do you enter into the divine love for all that exists? It is not so easy. Do you love snakes? But even if we are bitten by a snake, we ought to be able to love it at the very moment when we are bitten because the snake is not to blame, it is simply obeying an imperative of its instinct. The snake, like all nature, has been a victim of the Fall, but the Lord Love has not ceased to love it.

The most beautiful flower will die. This brings to mind the problems of dissolution and the end of things, of evil and death, of suffering and sin. All these are facts. A violent warfare is constantly being waged against Limitless Love. We shall return to this theme. But Love is a powerful wind, a hurricane that bursts windows open and smashes glass; it upsets entirely our preconceived ideas, it breaks the alabaster jar so that the perfume can be diffused, it is beyond the law, beyond and above what we call 'morality' and 'religion'. Love is victorious over death itself. All barriers are overcome by Limitless Love.

At this point, without further delay, I want to touch upon two very important matters which may have been troubling you. So far I have not spoken of the person of our Lord and Saviour Jesus Christ. Has not the humble, gentle figure of the Christ of the Gospels been lost in this ocean of Limitless Love? Was it necessary to have recourse to a transcendent conception of Love when, after all, it was through Love that God-made-man trod our earthly paths? May God preserve you from forgetting him who *is* Saving Love. I believe and I confess that Jesus was, and still is, the human countenance of

Limitless Love, and that in him there lives the fullness of divinity, and therefore of this very Love. But I dare to assert that here we shall be venturing 'beyond Jesus'. You must be quite clear what I mean by this. In a certain sense there is no such thing as 'beyond Jesus', for Jesus brought Infinity and Perfection into the world. But in another sense it is possible to go 'beyond Jesus' if by that we mean going beyond the historical figure of Jesus to attain to the Eternal Christ. In all Jesus said and did in public we must discover, we must discern, 'that which was within Jesus', the inner Jesus, the divine essence of Jesus. This divine essence was not limited to his person. Jesus himself prayed to God. In meditating upon the Limitless Love, we are reaching towards that which was a living spring in the Saviour's own soul.

The other point I must mention is the question of the inter-personal relationships at the heart of 'God-Love'. How can we speak of Limitless Love without contemplating the mystery of the Holy Trinity, of the three angels seated at Abraham's table, under the oak of Mamre? How can we ignore the distinction between the Father, his Son and his Spirit? I shall simply say that the richness and depth of this mystery are such that I would rather say nothing about them than speak of them too briefly and superficially. What I shall try to make clear is how Limitless Love is common to all three. You yourselves can explore further into the concept of Limitless Love. You can deepen the implications of the themes of the Lover, of the Beloved; of the 'Co-Lover', and of the 'Co-Beloved' in the same Love. You can reflect upon earthly analogies on the themes of love given, love received, and love shared (and this will greatly enlighten the role of the 'third man' in human affection towards a couple). You may, by this route, which is not the only one, be able to approach the mystery of Mamre, which is none other than the mystery of the Burning Bush under a different form. But this is not what I want to do here.

My aim, in this second meditation, has been to show that the flame of the Burning Bush represents the underlying link which is the secret of the universe; the living Love, concrete, intensely personal, which includes all men, all animals, all vegetation, all minerals, all planets, all space, and all the creations of which we have no knowledge. In the words of Dante 'That love which moves the sun and the other stars' is offered to every one of us. So we know now what we must call God, if we are going to venture as far as this into his heart. God is Limitless Love.

III

THE DOOR OF HOPE

And I will give her her vineyards from thence, and the valley of Achor for a door of hope. (Hosea 2:15)

As soon as we have spoken the words 'Limitless Love', or rather as soon as we have given a place in our hearts to this supreme reality, we have opened a door. It is the door that leads into the kingdom of liberty and light.

What is the meaning of this 'door of hope' of which the prophet Hosea speaks? The beginning of the book of Hosea is a strange but profound and moving parable. The Lord tells the prophet to take a prostitute to wife. Hosea does so. The woman abandons herself to a multitude of lovers. She does not find peace or happiness with them. God takes everything away from her, reducing her to a state of nakedness and dryness: 'I will lay waste her vines and her fig trees'.[1] Then the woman says, 'I shall go and return to my first husband'.[2] God sees her change of heart. He pardons her: 'Behold, I will allure her . . . and speak comfortably unto her'.[3] He restores the vines he had taken away, and transforms the valley of Achor into a door of hope. The importance of this change can be appreciated if we remember that the Hebrew word *achor* means 'trouble'. The valley of trouble becomes a door of hope for the forgiven soul.

The inner meaning of the story of Hosea, in its original context, obviously concerns the children of Israel. It relates to the spiritual prostitution and adulteries committed by the Hebrews, their violations of the precepts of Yaveh, their

[1] Hosea 2:12.   [2] Hosea 2:7.   [3] Hosea 2:14.

23

compromises with foreign idols, but it also shows Israel's repentance and the forgiveness granted by God—the forgiveness granted to the penitent adulteress 'as in the day when she came up out of the land of Egypt'.[4]

All this is a direct historical interpretation of the text. But the words that the Spirit spoke by the mouth of Hosea hold infinitely more than this particular meaning. The story of Hosea's wife is the story of each one of us. To each of us, however unfaithful we may have been to God, the Lord of Love opens the door of hope.

In the term 'door of hope' we find the conjunction of two words, two ideas. There is hope and there is the door. These two ideas have much in common; both of them express—the one psychologically, the other graphically—the idea of a threshold, an entrance, an introduction. Let us examine more closely what hope is, and what a door is.

Hope means first of all a period of waiting, of waiting for someone or something. It implies 'faith' in a certain kind of coming—in '*the* coming'. One does not know but one believes. It is a moral certainty, an inner certainty, not a scientific certainty. This waiting is inspired by love. Indeed love is its very foundation. One hopes only for what one loves. Thus hope is not only a matter of waiting. It is waiting permeated by love.

Here we must distinguish between our 'hopes'—in the plural—and our 'Hope' in the singular. I shall use the plural word for those particular things, those limited things, which we want to see happen, but which often merely signify our egotistical will. In this sense we may hope to recover from an illness, succeed in an enterprise, pass an examination. These are 'hopes'. But Hope is something quite different.

[4] Hosea 2 : 15.

24

Hope is a wish, a desire, a waiting, that has a bearing not merely upon a special object, but upon the whole of our destiny. There is the same difference between hopes and Hope as between sections of a curve and the curve in its entirety. If we consider only one part of the curve of our life, we may get an impression of failure, defeat, frustration. But we ought to be looking at the whole curve of our existence with a confidence inspired by love. Death itself, a moment of unique importance, is only a moment, a point, on the curve. The curve of our life is not an inverse curve. It is an outward curve, thrown outwards by our Creator towards the divine Limitlessness. We are not, by ourselves, limitless. Nothing created is limitless. But if we have received into ourselves the Love that is without limits, we have already become participants, by grace, of this divine Infinity.

What is the summit of Hope? It is the moment when we think that hope no longer exists, and when nevertheless we refuse to despair. Saint Paul spoke of Abraham 'who against hope believed in hope'.[5] Here we are touching upon the problem of suffering, so intimately linked with the ideas of Hope and of Limitless Love. I believe that the deepest response to the questions arising from human suffering and the existence of evil, not only human but cosmic, is given to us by the belief in a suffering God, a suffering Love. But you must be quite clear what I mean by this : there is no question of a diminished or defeated God. We are concerned with a victorious God who takes all human suffering on himself in order to surmount it, a God in whom the Passion and the Resurrection co-exist eternally, a God who is no stranger to any of our afflictions, who is indeed more intimately close to them than we ourselves. I wish I had time to reflect with you upon the theme of the suffering God and the supreme Pity.

[5] Romans 4 : 18.

But this is not the time or the place. I would simply like to remind you of two passages in Holy Scripture. One is about the three children whom King Nebuchadnezzar cast into the burning fiery furnace (and here we rediscover one of the aspects of the Burning Bush): 'Lo, I see four men loose, walking in the midst of the fire . . . and the form of the fourth is like the Son of God'.[6] And here is the other passage: 'Love is strong as death. . . . Many waters cannot quench love, neither can the floods drown it.'[7]

. Hope will cease to exist for those who, after death, see God. Faith and Hope will then pass away, and Love alone will remain. But during our earthly lives, during the time of our journey and our pilgrimage, Hope acts as a stimulant and an impetus to Love. We must stop thinking and speaking about our little individual hopes. Their disappointment is trivial compared to the limitless Hope which, because it springs from Limitless Love, can never be disappointed. Let us instead give ourselves to the power of this great Hope. When a stone is thrown into water the ripples radiate in ever wider and wider circles, and thus it is with Hope. If Hope sinks deep into us, its repercussions radiate through us to infinity.

Everlasting Hope is the hope of the dawn and the brightness of the morning. There is a difference between the way we ourselves count time and the way God counts it. We start our reckoning with the morning, with the joy of the sunrise, and our day proceeds towards the darkness, sadness, tragedy of night. But no less than six times in the first chapter of Genesis [8] God is shown as creating days which begin in the evening and progress towards morning and then high noon. This brings us back to the fullness of the light of the Burning

---

[6] Daniel 3:25. [7] Song of Songs 8: 6, 7.
[8] Gen. 1:5, 8, 13, 19, 23, 31.

Bush and of Limitless Love. Each day of our lives should consist of this progression from limited hopes and from a love threatened by death towards the brightness of the morning and the high noon of Limitless Love.

Now let us return, if you agree, to the book of Hosea, and to our text on the door of hope. You have already seen how Hope is the spontaneous reaction, the first response, to the discovery of Limitless Love. We enter into Limitless Love through the door of hope. This entrance means the beginning of possession, though not yet complete possession (and besides, it is Limitless Love who can possess us; we ourselves cannot be the possessors). And here I want to remind you of a text in the Book of Revelation, addressed to the Church of Philadelphia : 'Behold, I have set before thee an open door, and no man can shut it'.[9] These words are spoken to each one of us. Before each of us is opened Hosea's door of hope, and this is the very same door of which the Apocalypse tells, the door which no man can shut, which gives access to the Kingdom of Love.

What is this door? It is the door of the present opportunity, whatsoever that may be. Glancing back over the whole course of our lives, our chief impression may be of a succession of missed opportunities. Oh, if only I had known! Oh, if I had acted differently in those circumstances! Oh, if it could happen over again! But we cannot live our lives again. Admittedly there have been lost chances. They will not return. But these lost chances are as nothing compared to the new chances God will offer to us—compared to those he offers us at this very moment. And even though I should be given only one more chance before I die to seize a divine opportunity, so long as I *do* seize it this last-minute fulfil-

[9] Rev. 3 : 8.

ment will compensate for all the previous chances I have missed, will indeed annul them.

It is thus, so it seems to me, that one must understand the gospel parable of the five foolish virgins. They had missed their chance. They had been late: 'And the door was shut'.[10] How can we reconcile this stern parable with the compassionate saying about the door which is open before us, which no man can shut? The foolish virgins (and we ourselves, how often!) had been asleep, had left their lamps without oil, had missed the coming of the Bridegroom, had found themselves outside a closed door. Nevertheless, later on, new opportunities may have presented themselves to the foolish virgins, and to us God is offering them constantly.

Every day, at every moment, the door of hope opens before us. The resulting opportunity is different for each one of us. It may be that the door opens onto some exceptional task for which God has chosen us. But usually the opportunity or possibility brought to us by the present moment is not something spectacular and sensational. The door opens before us not so that we may do extraordinary deeds, but so that we may do the most ordinary things in an extraordinary way, thereby imparting to these ordinary things the temperature and the flame of the Burning Bush and the Love without limits.

The door is about to open before me now. It is now—never tomorrow—that I must go through it. Perhaps the door appears to be shut. But what a lamentable mistake to sit in front of it, merely looking at it, waiting for someone else to come and open it for me! I have only to push gently (the beginning of an effort, or at least an intention, is necessary on my own part) and it will open of itself. What am I saying? I need only advance towards it, and already it is

[10] Matt. 25 : 10.

opening of its own accord, like the automatic doors at an airport.

We must remind ourselves, however, that the door of hope is no more than an approach to Limitless Love. Participation in this same Love, in eternal life, is something quite different. There is a parallel here with engagement and marriage. The betrothal coincides in meaning with the door of hope. The ring is already placed on the finger of the betrothed. It is a time of joy. But Limitless Love calls us, from henceforth, to a closer union.

This brings us back once more to the prophet Hosea: 'I will give her . . . the valley of Achor for a door of hope, and she shall sing there, as in the days of her youth, and as in the day when she came up out of the land of Egypt. And it shall be at that day . . . that thou shalt call me Ishi, and shalt call me no more Baali.' [11] Baali means 'my master', Ishi means 'my husband'. From the moment when we pass through the door of hope, Limitless Love comes towards us. Is this Love still that immeasurable gift, the promised Love? No, it would be an understatement to say that. This Love is already the Love which is bestowed. Love says to us: 'From now on I shall no longer be thy master. Dost thou not desire me as thy husband? In this world our union will doubtless be very imperfect. Yet it is my own wish that thou shouldst call me "husband".'

[11] Hosea 2 : 15, 16.

IV

GREATLY BELOVED

*I am come to shew thee; for thou art
greatly beloved. (Daniel 9:23)*

During the time of the Jewish exile and the destruction of
Jerusalem the prophet Daniel was taking part in the evening
oblation. He was confessing his own sins and also the sins
of Israel. While thus in supplication before God he became
aware of the angel Gabriel (whom he had already seen in
another vision) advancing swiftly towards him. The angel
touched him and said: 'O Daniel, I am now come forth to
give thee skill and understanding. At the beginning of thy
supplications the commandment came forth, and I am come
to shew thee; for thou art greatly beloved: therefore understand the matter, and consider the vision.' [1]

The verses following those I have just quoted show that
the angel's mission and the divine message he brought to the
prophet were linked with future events at the time of the
coming of the Messiah. But in Daniel's vision, as in the vision
of the Burning Bush, God's message overflows and surpasses
the immediate historical context and has another meaning
which is universal and eternal. To explain this I want first of
all to take a phrase of only four words from the angel's
message: 'Thou art greatly beloved'. These words are
addressed to ourselves, to each one of us, just as much as to
Daniel. Let us try to discover their meaning. Let us apply to
this divine declaration the angel's command, 'Therefore
understand the matter, and consider the vision'.

[1] Daniel 9 : 22, 23.

Until very recently, whenever I had to speak in public of divine Love (and every priest should do so, whatever his own lack of love) I started by considering the love that man should have towards God. As my point of departure I readily took the Gospel precept 'Thou shalt love the Lord thy God . . .'.[2] But I am now convinced that a different approach is preferable. First place must be given to the Lord's love for men. We must begin at the beginning. We must never forget that man's love for God is no more than a response to God's love for men. Listen to the words of Saint John: 'Herein is love, not that we loved God, but that he loved us'.[3] Furthermore a fairly lengthy pastoral experience has taught me that it is difficult for a man to love God if he has not first of all been granted the revelation, the experience, of the love God has for him. At some point it is necessary to undergo the 'shock' of realising the passionate love God offers to us. God always takes the initiative. So I have now come to the conclusion that the way to announce the Gospel (at least in my own case) is to go directly towards men saying to each one of them 'Thou art beloved'. All else flows from that. It is the essential message.

'Thou art beloved. . . .' This declaration, this 'annunciation', leads us into the very midst of the Burning Bush. We are not only on the threshold of the mystery. We have indeed passed through the door of hope the prophet Hosea spoke of. At the moment when the Lord Love says 'Thou art beloved' we find ourselves within the very flames of the Bush, within the fire of Limitless Love. As yet we can be nothing more than wood that is green and wet, but if we pray to God we can (as the French put it so well) *prendre feu* —catch fire. At this initial stage we are like a man travelling through a dark winter's night, through a snowstorm. Sud-

2 Mark 12:30.   3 I John 4:10.

denly, amidst the snowflakes that freeze his hands he sees a light, several lights. Oh! Then there must be, quite nearby, a home with light, with warmth, a fire. . . . Limitless Love is calling us.

The Burning Bush is a cosmic love. Is there then in its flame a special place for my poor soul, for me, the lowest of all? Limitless Love is essentially personal. Coming from a personal God (or rather, so I should say with deeper meaning, from the three divine Persons of the Holy Trinity) Limitless Love flows out towards individual persons.

To be loved. . . . What does this mean, when God is the lover? Whatsoever our concept of love may be, all love is the movement of one being towards another, with a desire for some sort of union. The orientations of this movement and its forms and variants are innumerable. They range from the sub-human to the superhuman. But there is always a tendency towards union, a desire for union, either possessive or sacrificial. The love of God for men is a movement of God towards us, not merely so that we may know him, or (according to our ability) imitate him, but so that he may indeed give himself and unite himself to us.

God does not only say to us 'Thou art beloved', which means 'I wish to unite myself to thee'. He says to us, as to Daniel : 'Thou art *greatly* beloved', in other words, 'I greatly desire to unite myself to thee'. Let us linger here for a few moments on the significance of the two words 'greatly' and 'beloved'. In the word 'beloved' the prefix 'be-' already intensifies the word 'loved'. Yet expressions such as 'beloved' or 'greatly beloved' might incline us towards an emotional idea of the love which is limitless. You will probably be surprised and perhaps also shocked when I tell you that God cannot love much or little. Such words would imply certain limits to his love, and this would be the very negation of limitlessness. In God there is nothing quantitative. Love, insofar as it is the divine essence, is an absolute. There is within it neither more nor less. God simply loves. That is all. God gives himself. I would even avoid saying that God loves and gives himself 'totally' or loves all men 'equally'. For ideas of totality and equality lead us back to a quantitative notion of love. God loves 'divinely', which is to say that in every act of his love he communicates his indivisible being— and this means his limitlessness.

What? Does God love the sinner and the saint with the same love? Surely Holy Scripture would cry out in protest against such an idea? Surely the Bible speaks of men whom God loves, and of others from whom his love has been withdrawn? Admittedly the language of the Bible is a language of preferential love. But we must take two things into account; firstly that God, in revealing himself to men, has used methods and means of approach adapted to their intelligence, sometimes at a primitive stage—and at such a stage he speaks to them as a teacher, he gives them rules; secondly that the Bible abounds in anthropomorphisms, in human manners of speech. We ourselves are often forced to use a human vocabulary that includes very poor words, incapable of expressing divine realities.

Here I dare not lay down the law, but I *will* dare (for one must be audacious when speaking of Limitless Love) to put before you an idea and a symbol. Divine Love is comparable to the atmospheric pressure surrounding us, which sustains each being and also exerts pressure from all sides. Love lays siege to each being and seeks to discover an opening, a path leading into the heart, by means of which Love can permeate everywhere. The difference between the sinner and the saint is that the sinner closes his heart to Love while the saint

C

opens himself to this same Love. In both cases the Love is the same and the pressure is the same. The one rejects, the other accepts. (There is no acceptance without preliminary grace, but this grace was also offered to him who rejected it.) The difference does not come from God's side but from man's.

This comparison with atmospheric pressure may perhaps cause you uneasiness. Is divine Love merged then in some kind of ocean where everything is confused and lost? Far from it! I warned you against using 'preferential' language for Limitless Love. This Love is no chaos, no miasma. And although we should indeed avoid 'preferential' language we may and should speak of a 'differential' love, a radically differential love. This means that, while excluding all idea of the quantitative, we nevertheless admit that the Love of God for each being is radically different from the Love of God for every other being. In the domain of the absolute, in the domain of Limitless Love, circumstances are never twice the same. A particular case is never repeated. Every relationship of love between God and a particular man is exceptional and unique, and different in character from all the loving relationships between God and other men. There is never a 'more' or a 'less' but always a 'different'. Infinite Love is offered to each one. It lies with each one to open himself or to close himself to this divine gift. The Lord Love loves me as if I were the only person in the world, and he awaits my response as if my response alone were important.

'Thou art greatly beloved.' These words do not therefore mean 'Thou art loved more than others'. They mean 'Thou art loved divinely, thou art loved without limits, thou hast opened thyself to Love, and Love has taken possession of thee'. The words of Jesus 'Thou shalt love the Lord thy God

34

with all thy heart . . . ' can help us to understand the nature of God's love for us, because our human love is a reflection, an emanation, of God's love. Yet we cannot apply the words 'with all thy heart' quite literally to God's love, for that would involve quantitativeness; God's heart cannot be measured in terms of a whole, or a half, or a third. It is without limits. (Man's love has limits, because man himself is a finite creature.) Nevertheless we can use the expression 'with all thy heart' in a symbolic and inadequate way to express the idea that Love approaches us with immensity, infinity, absoluteness, limitlessness. Each of us and indeed every creature, even each microscopic grain of sand, is loved by God in a divine and overwhelming manner. If we take this seriously we shall indeed be overwhelmed. We are, at this very moment, infinitely small receiving points of Limitless Love. There is plenty in this thought to go to our heads, to overwhelm us. But God wants us to receive the declaration of his love with peace, humility, joy and confidence.

'Thou art beloved.' Notice the pronoun 'thou'. This declaration has nothing to do with a general or collective affirmation. God does not say 'You are beloved' in the plural. Certainly we are all of us the well-beloved of God. But in saying 'Thou art beloved' God speaks to the person who is myself, the 'me' whom he calls by a secret name (different from the name by which men know me), the name that is spoken of in the Apocalypse as 'written on a white stone' and which no one knows except the one who receives it. Each of us has the potentiality, and each may be given the opportunity, to discover a unique facet of the divine personality of the Lord who is also Love.

'Thou art greatly beloved.' Not 'thou wert' nor 'thou shalt be'. It is not yesterday or the day before that I have been loved. It is not tomorrow or the day after that I shall be loved but today, at this very moment. How, Lord? How can one who is in a state of sin be loved? Yea, Lord, I believe that thou never ceasest to love the sinner. Thou lovest all men, every man, whatever he may be, in whatever state he is. Lord, I give thee thanks for loving us after this fashion.

'Behold what manner of love the Father hath bestowed upon us.' [4] Together we have just been beholding this Love. 'Thou art beloved.' I pray that these divine words may remain in the depths of our hearts. And as we go on our way let us repeat them secretly, thereby revealing them to others, thereby letting them shine around us. 'Thou art greatly beloved.'

[4] I John 3 : 1.

V

THE WALLS OF JERICHO

*By faith the walls of Jericho fell down,
after they were compassed about seven
days.*

*By faith the harlot Rahab perished not
with them that believed not, when she
had received the spies with peace.*

(Hebrews 11:30, 31)

Can there be any sort of connection between the sombre story of Jericho and the radiant vision of the Burning Bush?

The biblical account of the fall of Jericho and the fate of its inhabitants—all of them massacred—raises serious and difficult problems, not only in the historical sense but also in the moral and religious senses. For the moment however we will leave all these problems aside. What concerns us now is to draw certain spiritual lessons from the story of Jericho, to understand certain things which the Spirit can say to us by means of it.

Jericho is the antithesis of the Burning Bush. It is the negation of everything the Bush stands for. The fire of the Burning Bush communicates itself, propagates itself, while Jericho is a closed city, rejecting all outside contacts. Jericho is limitation affirming itself as such, and opposing itself to Limitless Love.

The Jericho that Joshua was to seize was a fortress-town lying between Jerusalem and the Jordan. Not only was it surrounded by high walls, intended for defence against all attack, but there was a double ring of walls (this has been revealed by recent excavations). Jericho had no wish to receive the children of Israel. Indeed all contact with the outside world was forbidden. 'Now Jericho was straitly shut up. . . . None went out, and none came in.' [1]

This is what Jericho was in the past. What is Jericho now? I do not mean the contemporary town which we can visit between Jerusalem and Jordan, nor do I mean the sites that have proved so fruitful for the archaeologists. I mean the ever-present spiritual Jericho, the symbolic Jericho, the universal Jericho. This Jericho is you and me. Jericho means ourselves if we have cut ourselves off from loving relationships and built up barriers against the demands of Limitless Love.

There are two ways in which this Jericho can manifest itself. Sometimes we see Jericho in another person, or in a group of people, whom we want to approach, and with whom we would like to enter into a genuine and loving relationship. But Jericho closes its gates to us. What can be done? Should we stage an assault on the ramparts? No. Rather we should do what the Hebrews did: we should repeatedly compass the city about, bearing with us the Ark of the Lord—this means all that is most sacred to us—meanwhile remaining in silence except for the sound of the liturgical trumpets. And this must continue until the Lord says to us, as he said to Joshua: 'I have given into thine hand Jericho'.[2] Perhaps we shall reach the end of our lives without having seen the success of this patient siege, the surrender of those for whose love we have prayed. But within, hidden from sight, we have, so much as in us lies, destroyed the wall by means of our one-sided love. Let us trust in God that he will cause this love to bring about its effect, also from within, upon the other person.

[1] Joshua 6: 1.   [2] Joshua 6: 2.

But this aspect of the fall of Jericho is not the one I want to make the primary theme of our meditation. Rather I would like to consider with you the situation when we ourselves have built up defences against love.

The walls of Jericho were not built in a day. Such fortifications took years. It is often because of a slow accumulation of secreted matter that an ear becomes deaf. In the same way, it is stone by stone, day by day, year by year, that we have built up our wall of egoism, ever higher and higher. We have even cut ourselves off, as Jericho did, by two enclosing walls: the ramparts visible to all, our negative words and actions, and the even more disastrous invisible rampart, our thoughts which are obstinately centred upon ourselves.

This process of estrangement and separation, of cutting ourselves off, contradicts the very trend of biological evolution. Think of the primaeval creatures with their thick defensive shells. Those shells have gradually gone. And when creatures lost their heavy defences they developed nervous systems. Evolution means an opening up of communication and contact. Attempts to cut ourselves off are against the meaning of the universe. They are sinful. Unloving separation, whatever form it may take, is a sin. Separation is *the* sin. And Jericho may therefore be regarded as a symbol of sin, insofar as it stands for separation. This Jericho, our Jericho, who is laying siege to it? God is besieging it, and so are other men. The besieger is Love.

Joshua was commanded to take Jericho in an extraordinary manner. 'By faith the walls of Jericho fell down.' The Hebrews had to assemble and make procession round the city carrying the Ark of the Covenant. No word was uttered. But the trumpet and the ram's horn were blown. This was to continue for six days. On the seventh day the walls of Jericho disintegrated.

Jericho is not a fortress to be conquered by methods of war. Love does not mount an assault on our souls. Nor can we ourselves destroy our own walls. We cannot take them down stone by stone. But the Lord Love compasses us about patiently, repeatedly. The sound of the trumpets is the call of Limitless Love. Love erodes our deepest inner defences. And then God shakes the foundations and our Jericho falls apart.

Archaeological researches at Jericho confirm the biblical account. The walls were not demolished by human effort but there are traces of an earthquake, of a 'shaking of the foundations'. Such a trembling of the earth was also needed, says the Gospel, to roll away the stone that closed the tomb of our Lord. Small adjustments are not enough to liberate; there must be profound upheavals.

The archaeologists have also found traces of a fire at Jericho. The earthquake probably caused this fire (the striking of one stone against another causes a spark). The soul, after the first great tremor, bursts into flame. The fire at Jericho, the historic Jericho, but also at our own Jericho, brings us back to the flames of the Burning Bush.

The ram's horn was sounded when the walls fell. This has an important symbolism. For the Jews the ram, and therefore its horn, signified ritual sacrifice. And still on Yom Kippur (the Day of Atonement) the sounding of a ram's horn within the synagogue announces the forgiveness of sins. To the Fathers of the Church the immolation of the ram was a symbol of Christ's sacrifice. Christ is present every time a wall of partition is abolished, at Jericho or anywhere else. 'For he is our peace', as Saint Paul says, 'who hath made both one, and hath broken down the middle wall of partition

40

between us'.[3] This same Christ pronounces over us the same marvellous words he addressed to the man who was deaf and had an impediment in his speech: 'Ephphatha, that is, Be opened'.[4]

'Be opened. . . .' Those words lead me to give you, in passing, some other quotations. First of all here is something contemporary, a striking phrase that was spoken by the founder of the Oxford Group and the Moral Re-Armament movement: 'Let the whole world march into your heart'. But chiefly I want to draw your attention to two other texts from Holy Scripture: 'My son, give me thine heart' [5] and 'A new heart also will I give you, and a new spirit will I put within you: and I will take away the stony heart out of your flesh and I will give you an heart of flesh'.[6] At the present time heart transplants provide us with a wonderful symbol. In a symbolical sense they represent the antithesis to the 'closed' attitude of Jericho. Furthermore prior to the operation the whole organism has to be prepared to receive the new heart. In the possibility of changing physical hearts we can see a parable—a beautiful parable—of the triumph of Limitless Love.

I must now say a few words about the second part of our text. You will remember that it reads as follows: 'By faith the harlot Rahab perished not with them that believed not, when she had received the spies with peace'. The Rahab episode is very important. Two soldiers had been sent by Joshua to spy out the inner defences of Jericho. These men managed to enter the forbidden city. They came into the house of a harlot called Rahab and lodged there. Everything seems to suggest that they spent the night with her.

3 Eph. 2 : 14.   4 Mark 7 : 34.
5 Prov. 23 : 26.   6 Ezekiel 36 : 26.

The King of Jericho was aware of this and sent an order to Rahab to hand over the men. But Rahab hid them, denied any knowledge of where they came from, and finally helped them to escape outside the walls. Before they left they agreed with her that in return for her kindness she and her whole family would be spared, when the time came for the Lord to give the land of Jericho to the Hebrews. A scarlet thread bound in the window would be a sign of recognition. And so it came about. When all the people of Jericho were slaughtered 'Joshua saved Rahab the harlot alive',[7] and all her household with her.

This is not a very moral story, in the conventional sense of the word. Rahab is a prostitute, she disobeys the orders of her king, she tells a lie, she commits an act of treason. Yet she has God's blessing. The psalmist says: 'Glorious things are spoken of thee, O city of God. I will make mention of Rahab.' [8] The apostle James, in his Epistle, compares her to Abraham and writes: 'Likewise also was not Rahab the harlot justified by works, when she had received the messengers, and had sent them out another way'.[9] And in the Epistle to the Hebrews, the text upon which we are meditating speaks of Rahab as having been saved by faith when she received the spies with peace.

Saved by faith? What faith? It was not a very clear or explicit faith. But Rahab herself admitted that she did not ignore the miraculous escape of the children of Israel from Egypt. She had a confused intuition that divine help had been granted to Israel. But the point I want to stress here is that her faith was expressed in her 'works' by means of an act bearing witness to Limitless Love.

Jericho was a self-limited city, refusing all outside contacts; Rahab violated its limitations and helped not only

7 Joshua 6 : 25. 8 Ps. 87 : 3, 4. 9 James 2 : 25.

strangers but enemies. She stands for the love that rebels against restrictions and will not admit them. She shows herself kind, compassionate and generous. And, before God, Rahab's compassion for the two soldiers counted for more than the irregularity of her life.

May one not see a prophetic allusion in the detail of the scarlet thread, which for Rahab was a sign and instrument of grace. Isaiah was later to say: 'Though your sins be as scarlet, they shall be as white as snow; though they be red like crimson, they shall be as wool'.[10] And Saint Mark's Gospel, in the description of our Lord in the Hall of Judgment, was to include the words 'and they clothed him with purple' [11]—the red of the saving Passion.

But the divine paradox, the blessed scandal, blazes out to the uttermost in the direct link which exists between Rahab and Jesus. He who accepted the tears, the kisses, and the anointing of the woman who was a sinner, he who dismissed without words of reproach the woman taken in adultery, he who declared to the chief priests that the publicans and harlots would go into the Kingdom of God before them,[12] he it was who admitted that Rahab should be included in his own genealogy [13]; Limitless Love wished that, in his earthly incarnation, his name should be formally linked with that of a prostitute.

[10] Isaiah 1 : 18.   [11] Mark 15 : 17.   [12] Matt. 21 : 31.   [13] Matt. 1 : 5.

VI

CLEAN AND UNCLEAN

What God hath cleansed, that call not thou common. (Acts 10:15)

When Peter was lodging at Joppa with Simon, a tanner, whose house was by the seaside, he went up onto the housetop to pray at about the sixth hour. He fell into a trance and saw heaven opened 'and a certain vessel descending unto him, as it had been a great sheet knit at the four corners . . . wherein were all manner of four-footed beasts of the earth, and wild beasts, and creeping things, and fowls of the air'. A voice said to him 'Rise, Peter, kill and eat'. But Peter answered 'Not so, Lord, for I have never eaten any thing that is common or unclean'. Then the voice spoke to him again saying: 'What God hath cleansed, that call not thou common'. This vision of Peter's related directly to a great problem confronting the Church at its very birth. Should she be the Church of certain people only, the Church of the privileged Jews, or should she throw herself open to the Gentiles, to those who did not belong to Israel?

In the meantime, in Caesarea, a Roman centurion called Cornelius, who feared God and gave generously to the poor, had seen a vision of an angel telling him to send to Joppa for Peter. When his messengers found Peter he received them and accompanied them to Caesarea. The apostle then conferred with Cornelius and his friends. He realised that his vision of the clean and unclean creatures had been a sign: God is no respecter of persons, and all who work righteousness—Jews and Gentiles alike—are accepted by him. Peter broke the news of Jesus to this group of Gentiles. The Holy Spirit fell upon all of them, and they received baptism at Peter's hands.

The episode at Joppa has a wider and deeper significance than the admission of Gentiles into the Christian community. Its immediate meaning, at the time, concerned the relationship between the conventionally pure—the Jews— and the conventionally impure—the Gentiles. But the problem it raises is a far greater one. For it also concerns the relationship of pure and impure in the widest possible sense.

At the beginning of these addresses I told you that Horeb and Sinai, different parts of the same mountain, corresponded to two different ethics, that of the Burning Bush and that of the Tables of the Law. There is an unavoidable conflict between the ethic of the Burning Bush, of Limitless Love, and the ethic of the Ten Commandments. Admittedly Horeb and Sinai may both at the same time inspire a human life. But it is perhaps easier to keep resolutely to one or the other of the two attitudes. Mixing the two may create difficulties. For example, if we assume the viewpoint of the Law when considering the story of Rahab (to which I drew your attention in the last address) we may be not a little disconcerted to find that our generally accepted morality does not always coincide with the divine ethic. Let us ask ourselves then what *is* the ethic of the Burning Bush, the ethic of Limitless Love?

For a start Limitless Love rejects a moral attitude which is strictly legalistic. By that I mean an attitude concentrated on the letter of the law, on precepts and prohibitions. But over and above this Limitless Love abolishes the Law. I hope I do not scandalise you. Let me remind you that I am not alone in speaking thus of the abolition of the Law. Listen to the words of one of the apostles, Saint Paul: 'Ye are not under the law, but under grace' [1]; 'Now we are delivered from the law' [2]; 'Christ is the end of the law'. [3]

But we must be quite clear what these texts mean. Every divine commandment is just and good. That which God has called evil remains evil. It is possible to live a holy life by keeping strictly to the Ten Commandments, or by following the inspiration of the Epistle of Saint James (which furthermore is animated by an intense fraternal charity) rather than by following the Epistles of Saint Paul and Saint John. Murder, impurity, egoism, are sins today just as they were yesterday.

What then is new? This is what is new. If today we abstain from killing, stealing, lying, committing adultery, it is no longer (I am here speaking from a specifically Christian angle) because these things have been the subject of prohibitions written on tables of stone, but because 'someone' has lived in a certain way and has died in a certain way. Here let us turn again to Saint Paul: 'He is our peace . . . having abolished in his flesh the enmity, even the law of commandments contained in ordinances'. [4] It is extraordinary that these words should have found so few echoes among traditional Christians, who persist in seeing the Gospel through Old Testament eyes.

The person of Jesus and the life of Jesus have replaced the Commandments. The intimate and profound significance of each of the Commandments remains, but the letter has given place to the spirit. When a river flows into the sea, each drop of the river's water continues to exist in the sea, but the river, as a river, no longer exists. And how its drops of water are transformed in that immense ocean! It is thus with the Commandments of Sinai, when they melt in the flames of the Burning Bush, in the fire of Limitless Love.

[1] Romans 6:14.   [2] Romans 7:6.   [3] Romans 10:4.
[4] Eph. 2:14, 15.

At the present time the strong reaction against a legalistic concept of Christianity, a reaction in itself very valid (for all is grace), sometimes dissipates itself in blind alleys. The idea of an 'ethic of situation' is widespread. Such an ethic refuses to accept universal principles. Nothing matters except the circumstances of each situation. It confines itself to the particular case, to the concrete 'situation' existing at the present moment. It ignores everything else. Such a morality is not acceptable from the viewpoint of Limitless Love. For all such ethics of situation are inevitably like boats without sails, without oars, without compasses, at the mercy of winds and waves. Anyone who refuses to look beyond the present situation runs the risk of becoming no more than an instrument of his own conscious or subconscious desires.

But if on the one hand we reject a legalistic morality, a code based on the letter of the law, and on the other hand a morality of situation, what are we to do when faced by practical problems? We must find a criterion for action surpassing both the written law and the isolated case. We must discover not another law but a 'principle' which is transcendent and at the same time universal, which can illuminate every situation and yet is flexible enough to adapt itself to particular circumstances. The ethic of Limitless Love fulfils both these demands. It surpasses all legal precepts but it also surpasses all individual cases. It does not lead us to consult written rules but instead offers us an inspiration and a sense of direction. It has a fixed centre, a constantly glowing heart, but there are as many different nuances in the way we apply it as there are different beams of light shining out from its radiance.

This is not the moment to go into every aspect of the ethic of Limitless Love. Rather let us concentrate on the essential command 'Thou shalt love'. Nevertheless I would like to draw your attention to a few things which seem to me fundamental. First of all, if we want to look at a moral problem through the eyes of love we must look at it in full daylight. This means that we must ask ourselves what there is, in this particular situation, that is true, authentic. A situation can seem 'regular' in the eyes of men while remaining far from regular in the eyes of God. A relationship may appear valid according to ecclesiastical law while before God it is invalid. Conversely a situation regarded by men as irregular may be regular before God. This should always be borne in mind in matrimonial cases (marriage, divorce, adultery etc.). In such cases it is the inner truth, the intention, the consent, that matters, over and above even the most correct of exterior forms, and indeed sometimes in contradiction of them. 'For the letter killeth, but the spirit giveth life.' [5]

An ethic of Love is incompatible with offences against love. Thus it cannot justify or absolve the deliberate infliction of suffering, unless the suffering is obviously in the highest interests of the person concerned. When we ourselves are faced with the prospect of suffering, which would come to us as the result of such or such a moral decision, it often happens that acceptance of the suffering is the criterion of the best solution. In most cases the best solution is that which involves a real sacrifice on our own part, because sacrifice, the sacrifice transcending reason, is the most profound expression of love.

The ethic of Limitless Love demands that we should be able to recognise the presence of God in the very sin that the sinner commits. Let us be very precise here. You must not think I mean that God approves of the sin or en-

[5] II Cor. 3 : 6.

courages the sinner. I simply mean that even in an act of sin God is, to a certain extent, present. This does not mean only that God, while condemning the sinful act, continues to love the sinner himself. There is more to it than that. On the one hand, everything that happens the bad act as well as the good—has its roots in the being of God. Only because God gives us our being (or rather lends it to us) are we in existence at the very moment when we commit a sin. At that very moment God could withdraw our being from us, could destroy us. But he holds us in the existence we have received from him, even when that existence turns against him. Moreover the Lord Love, in his infinite mercy, allows sin to contain certain positive elements. Let us take a common example. A man enters into sexual relations with a prostitute. If at any point during their intercourse the man or the woman experiences something other than egotistical desire, if, even for a quarter of an hour, even for a minute, he or she has a genuine feeling of tenderness, of disinterested self-giving, or perhaps of compassion, then, though we cannot claim that this spark from the Burning Bush has abolished that which, in this act, was contrary to the Lord Love or has had a redeeming effect upon the whole act, we *can* say that Limitless Love has entered into it, has infiltrated the sinful act and has left there a potent seed which can extend itself, can penetrate the soul and produce there, later on, fruits of salvation. The important thing then is to recognise the presence of God within a guilty act and to adore this presence, at the same time separating it radically from that which, in the same act, is alien or contrary to Limitless Love. What this all means, in fact, is that we should give thanks to God for showing forth his compassion in ways that are so often unexpected and always new.

What attitude should the ethic of Love inspire in the case

D

of a sinner who is conscious of his sin, and even laments it, but lacks the strength to give it up? We all know such cases. First of all the sinner must place himself honestly before God in the full light of truth, without seeking to excuse himself or belittle his faults, but declaring himself a sinner, powerless to change his situation by himself, submitting himself to the judgment and grace of God. Sin remains sin. White remains white and black black. But it is here that the Church can intervene in a specially helpful way. And, in this kind of case, so I dare to claim, the Eastern Churches show themselves especially compassionate. When confronted by an apparently desperate situation they know how to transfer the problem from the moral plane to the pastoral and personal plane. They cannot declare that evil is good. They cannot justify sin. But they can act with a certain patience, can avoid sudden solutions which might bring about catastrophic results for a soul or perhaps for two souls. He who assumes the grave responsibility of a 'spiritual father'—or, if you like, a 'universal brother'—will say to the weak and unfortunate sinner: 'Admit before God your responsibility as a sinner. There must be no compromise in your heart. Place before Limitless Love the limits that you do not know how to break away from. Stay in touch with me. Whatever may be your sin, my brother or my sister, and even if Absolute Love cannot absolve you at this moment, I shall not abandon you, I will not throw you overboard. I will enter into your diffi-culties. Let us pray together. Let us beg God to lead us to the solution that we cannot yet find.'

In short, the ethic of Love—or rather the spirituality of Love—knows how to set aside, when necessary, the search for the most just theoretical solution, in favour of a search for that which is best for the soul concerned. It is in Love that salvation can be found. If I want to help a sinner to leave his sin, I try, in my poor way, to act as God acts in respect of this sinner and this sin; in other words I try to love him, or her, out of it.

To love, with all one's heart, as oneself; the Gospel transmutes all of the law and the prophets into that. 'Thou shalt love the Lord thy God with all thy heart, and with all thy soul, and with all thy mind. . . . Thou shalt love thy neighbour as thyself.' [6] This gives us a standard truly according to the Gospel for all good thought, all good speech, all good acts: do I, in admitting this thought, in speaking these words, in making this action, love the Lord Love with all my heart and my neighbour as myself? I will not say 'This is so easy!'. But I will say 'It is so simple!'. It is all a question of integrity. It is a matter of offering our whole heart to Love, a heart which is pure as a wine is pure, a heart unadulterated and whole, a heart which is not divided or shared. And in the light of this it might perhaps be useful to revise our contemporary understanding of purity, or more precisely of chastity. Too often we think of chastity in negative terms, as no more than a matter of abstaining. But a chaste heart, a pure heart, is a whole heart, an integrated, total, heart which offers itself to God or to men in its wholeness. The real sin against purity is to offer (or to seem to offer) to God, or to a man, or to a woman, a love which is falsified, a love that is not or cannot be integral, a heart that is not 'whole'.

Have we been drifting away from the text with which we began this meditation? No. Peter's vision at Joppa, and the divine words 'What God hath cleansed, that call not thou common' have been behind everything we have been saying. This vision and these words convey to us the attitude towards

6 Matt. 22:37, 39.

sin and the sinner inspired by the Burning Bush and Limit-less Love. The unclean creatures in the great sheet Peter saw represent all which can seem to us 'unclean'. This means—to mention only a few of the aberrations especially in evidence in our own day—drug addiction, homosexuality and abor-tion. Faced by such things are we going to say, as Peter did, 'No, Lord, may it be far from me'? The Lord Love replies: 'There are, among these particular things, some I have already purified entirely. Others I am purifying at this moment. But I cannot purify or pardon without an inner change in the sinners. I ask you to participate in my work of purification by your prayer, by your sympathy for the sinner (not for the sin), by your adoring discovery of my absolute Purity acting secretly in the very midst of the visible impurity, so that it shall be consumed in my flame. To you, as to Peter, I say "Kill and eat".' 'Kill' here means 'Separate the entirely negative element from the positive element existing in all faults. Cut it off as with a sword.' And 'eat' means 'Assimilate everything which in the sinner comes from me and continues to be mine, and unite yourself to me in my effort to transfigure that which is not of me. Enlarge your heart to the dimensions of my heart.'

I believe without any reservation that Limitless Love is always at work to make clean that which was unclean. And I repeat with Saint Peter, 'God hath shewed me that I should not call any man common or unclean'.[7]

[7] Acts 10 : 28.

VII

A GREAT FIRE

And the barbarous people showed us no
little kindness: for they kindled a fire,
and received us every one. (Acts 28:2)

Now we have come to the last of our meditations. The incident referred to in the above text is a living, striking
example of what the Burning Bush, in other words, Limitless Love, can bring to pass among us.

You will remember that Saint Paul, with some other
prisoners, had been put on board a ship, under an escort of
Roman soldiers, to be taken from Palestine to Rome. They
were going to be tried before Caesar. In the Acts of the
Apostles you will find the story of the vicissitudes of that
voyage. The prisoners had to endure both storms and hunger.
They were shipwrecked. They managed to escape with their
lives when the escorting soldiers wanted to kill them. And
finally they got ashore onto the island of Malta.

Paul had played a major part in all this. He had helped
in the handling of the ship. He had inspired courage in his
despairing companions (who were not Christians). Without
ostentation, without seeking to proselytise, he had given
thanks to God before eating. And an angel had said to him
'Lo, God hath given thee all them that sail with thee'.[1] What
a wonderful assurance which we ourselves may well envy!
Oh if we could only truly believe that God has—to a certain
extent—entrusted to our care those around us. And what a
marvellous light this throws upon what could be, in the

[1] Acts 27:24.

53

communal needs of daily life, a peaceful co-existence, a wholehearted partnership, between the disciples of Christ and men who are ignorant of the Gospel or enemies to it.

So Paul and the other prisoners—there were more than two hundred of them—had escaped from the wreck onto the island of Malta. And there the local inhabitants lit a fire for them, and showed them 'no little kindness'. Those three short words are an understatement loaded with deep meaning. The Maltese gave the refugees a welcome which was very far from half-hearted, indeed they showed a humaneness quite out of the ordinary. And what was so outstanding, so extraordinary, in their welcome? The people of Malta had allowed the survivors of the wreck to land, but they were under no obligation to do more. They were not compelled to light a fire. And the exceptional quality of the way they received the strangers becomes more apparent if we consider who the welcomers were and who the welcomed.

The Maltese were barbarians—'the barbarous people'. This term 'barbarians', used by Saint Paul himself, shows clearly what a gulf existed between the islanders and the more or less 'official' shipload of people who had just come ashore. A barbarian was, in Roman eyes, a man who could speak neither Latin nor Greek, a man whose civilisation was inferior to that of the Empire. But the barbarians of Malta were generous, more generous than the soldiers who had thought of killing the prisoners, more generous than the sailors who had tried to save their own skins by abandoning the ship in distress as well as those on board.

And who were the newcomers to Malta? On the one hand there were the Roman soldiers, on the other the prisoners. Prisoners . . . people who were going to be tried, who had been accused of crimes. Was there no adverse prejudice against them? Did such people really deserve a friendly reception? Was it worth the trouble of making a fire for them? Surely there were prisons on the island which would be the normal place to put them? And as for the soldiers, responsibility for their welfare belonged to the Roman Empire. Surely they could find lodging on the island in guardhouses, or barracks, or inns?

You see what a paradox there is in the welcome that the people of Malta gave to the shipwrecked survivors. 'No little kindness' . . . this is where Limitless Love begins. Here is the spirit of the Gospel. Jesus once asked his listeners what they did that was out of the ordinary: 'What do ye more than others?'.[2] The charity of the Maltese represents a beginning. Higher still in the scale is the attitude of the Samaritan who, when leaving the wounded Jew he had succoured, gave money to the inn-keeper and said: 'Take care of him; and whatsoever thou spendest more, when I come again, I will repay thee'.[3] 'Whatsoever'—a blank cheque. Nearly all the gospel parables call us towards this 'whatsoever'; they call us to transcend limits, indeed to turn limits upside down.

In the case of the people of Malta, their 'no little kindness' found immediate expression in the lighting of a great fire. You note I say a *great* fire. Many translations of the Greek text omit the word 'great'. They simply say that the barbarous people 'lit a fire' or 'kindled a fire'. But other translations speak of a 'great fire', and to me this seems more accurate, for the original Greek word does not signify simply 'a fire'. It suggests a fairly large bonfire. Furthermore it is hard to imagine that anyone would be content to light a paltry fire to warm the survivors from a shipwreck. A real blaze was needed.

Here, yet again, we discover the Burning Bush. The Bush

[2] Matt. 5 : 47.   [3] Luke 10 : 35.

that flamed on Horeb was also a great blaze. It was no flickering little fire. Limitless Love exists only at a high temperature—a high temperature that does not in any way signify feverish disorder but rather a state of radiant fervour. And it demands that we should, so to speak, 'take our temperature' several times every day, that we should maintain within ourselves this state of dynamic fervency. 'Did not our heart burn within us?' [4]

We cannot remain within the Burning Bush unless we are constantly communicating to others the flame of which we are the carriers (and this is possible even when 'the other' is not physically present). The Book of Acts tells us what were the specific needs of those for whom the people of Malta lit their fire: 'Because of the present rain, and because of the cold'.[5] Two fundamental needs, we might almost say two different kinds of men, are indicated here. Some men are supremely sensitive to shocks from the outside, to the drenching caused by rain, to the external enemy. Others are more susceptible to interior cold, to a persistent lack of warmth in the soul. We should therefore give both shelter and warmth; we should help those who suffer from outward misfortunes and also those who suffer from interior sadness.

The Maltese did more than light a fire to warm the ship-wrecked. This fire was probably lit on the beach. But was such a fire alone enough? Could one leave people in distress on the seashore, without any help except a fire? No: in the words of the Book of Acts: 'They received us every one'.[6] This statement goes much further than all before it. Literally, in a practical sense, it means that Paul and his companions were received into the people's homes; the fact that the writer says 'us' suggests that he himself was one of these

[4] Luke 24 : 32.   [5] Acts 28 : 2.
[6] Acts 28 : 2.

56

companions and gives the narrative a vivid ring of truth. And from the spiritual viewpoint the phrase is very rich in meaning. Limitless Love 'receives'. Limitless Love receives into the home—into our own home, into Love's own home. He receives, not by a formal gesture, but by offering a genuine and friendly welcome. He receives 'every one' without exception. He opens all doors. 'Lift up your heads, O ye gates; and be ye lift up, ye everlasting doors.' [7]

And now we have reached the end of these addresses. I will leave with you a thought inspired by the great fire that was offered to those survivors by the 'barbarians' of Malta. If we are truly servants of the Lord Love, if the Burning Bush is given to us as a symbol of faith and a sign of action, we must go down to the seashore to meet the shipwrecked, we must go out into the streets towards those whom the rain has soaked and the cold has paralysed. With us we shall take a glowing brazier to kindle everywhere a new fire. And each evening we shall ask ourselves: 'Today, what limits have I overcome? What doors have I opened to the King of Glory, to Limitless Love? Today, what fire have I lighted, what fire do I want to light, for whom shall I light a fire?' In the words of Limitless Love 'I am come to send fire on the earth'.[8]

[7] Ps. 24 : 7.   [8] Luke 12 : 49.

NOTES

1. *The biblical episode of the Burning Bush*

The question of the historical validity of this episode will not be raised here, for in these pages it is treated exclusively as a theme and a symbol concerning the spiritual life. The passage in Exodus 3 has been dealt with in detail in rabbinical and Talmudic writings under the heading 'Concerning the Bush'. And besides, there are relevant references in Luke 20:37 and Mark 12:26. The words in the Greek text are: *epi tou batou.*

2. *The topography of the Burning Bush*

It is impossible and useless to try to identify or discuss the place where the episode occurred. The traditional site is within the Greek Orthodox monastery of Saint Catherine on Sinai. Some years ago, to remind pilgrims of the Burning Bush, the monks were still showing them a garden planted with bramble bushes. The Hebrew word for 'bush' (in the Bible) is *seneh.* This word designates all kinds of thorny plants.

3. *The Angel of Jehovah*

The angel who appeared to Moses in the Bush was an anthropomorphic manifestation of God; many such manifestations are mentioned in the Bible, in a variety of contexts. Saint Stephen, in recalling the incident of the Burning Bush, referred sometimes to the being who appeared to Moses as an angel, sometimes simply as God.[1]

4. *The Valley of Achor—Door of Hope*

It is not idle to dwell upon the striking contrast between Hope and the Valley of Achor. This valley, in Hebrew *emeq Achor,* was the place where, on the orders of Joshua, the stoning of Achan took place—the stoning of the man who had sacrilegiously appropriated part of the spoil from the capture of Jericho. Achan's

[1] Acts 7:31-35.

family was stoned with him.[2] The name of the valley, 'Achor', from the root *achar* 'to trouble', related to this event. In the memory of the Hebrews the place had remained an accursed one. Yet Isaiah said that this door of affliction would be changed into a pasture for herds,[3] a sign of peace and tranquillity, and with Hosea it became a symbol of hope.

5. *Rahab*

Despite the attempts at rehabilitation made by several Jewish writers, for example Josephus, (they have tried to make out that Rahab was a respectable inn-keeper) the rabbinical literature confirms the epithet *zonah*, 'prostitute', (*porne* in the Septuagint) which is used in the Bible. In Aramaic she has even been called *pandekita*, a transcription of the Greek *pandokissa*, 'she who gives herself to all'. Rahab married Salmon, son of Naasson, and was the mother of Booz, an ancestor of David. And without going into the problems relating to the gospel genealogies of Jesus, it must be pointed out that the inclusion of Rahab in them is no more amazing than the inclusion of Tamar and Bathsheba. But Rahab holds a privileged place in the Judeo-Christian tradition. Clement, Justin, Irenaeus, Origen and Jerome all develop the symbolism of the scarlet thread as a sign of redemption. A rabbinical tradition says that the conversion and faith of Rahab were so profound that they evoked the admiration of God himself.

6. *The pastoral attitude towards the sinner in the Eastern Churches*

What is said here about the indulgence shown in the Eastern spiritual tradition, not towards sin but towards the person of the sinner himself, is illustrated by the manner in which the Orthodox Churches regard problems of a sexual nature. It is well known that the canon law of the Eastern Churches admits divorce fairly freely (even if the marriage was originally valid) because of a kind of compassion, yet it does not lose sight of the ideal of a permanent conjugal union. The most significant text in connection

[2] Joshua 7.   [3] Isaiah 65 : 10.

with this pastoral tolerance is perhaps the twenty-sixth 'Canon of Saint Basil', one of the eighty-five canons quoted by Basil in his three letters to Bishop Amphilochius of Iconium, written in 374–375. This text, relating not to marriage but to concubinage, may astonish or even scandalise some readers. Here is the text : 'Fornication is not marriage; it is not even the beginning of marriage. That is why, if it is possible to induce those who have united themselves in fornication to separate, this is the best thing to do. But if they desire absolutely to live together, the penance reserved for fornication shall be imposed on them, yet without separating them, lest something worse should result.'

7. *The great fire at Malta*

There is no point in trying to deduce, from the original Greek text, the nature and dimensions of the fire that was lighted at Malta for the shipwrecked survivors. The versions that speak simply of 'a fire' would be correct if the Greek word from which they were translated were *pyr*, for this means, precisely, 'fire'. But the Greek word is *pyra*. And *pyra* means a mass of material in flames. It also means a funeral pyre. Thus it certainly means 'a *great* fire'. It is interesting to notice, too, that Herodotus uses the word *pyra* to designate an altar for burnt offerings. That fire which was lit by the people of Malta for the refugees; was it not, in its deepest reality, a burnt offering to Charity?

8. *The reception of the shipwrecked into the houses*

Paul himself received hospitality from Publius, the principal representative of Roman authority on the island of Malta. The other survivors may have been put under *custodia militaris*, a condition which permitted a prisoner to live in a private house provided he was handcuffed to a soldier. This applied in the case of Paul in Rome.[4] Or possibly Publius organised some kind of common lodging for the other prisoners. There is great spiritual importance in the response Paul made to the charity of the

4 Acts 28 : 16.

Maltese; he laid hands on the sick and healed them. What are our own deep responses to the welcomes from which we benefit?

9. *Representations of the Burning Bush*

The theme of the Burning Bush has naturally attracted the attention of painters. It has been portrayed by Raphael, Poussin, and Le Brun, but most notably by Nicolas Froment (1435–1484). His famous triptych, now in Aix Cathedral, links the Virgin Mother with the Burning Bush. The bush that is burning is shown in the form of trees, and the tree-tops—a mass of flowers and leaves—form a crown. At the centre of the crown Mary is seated with the Holy Child in her arms. Perhaps this idea inspired Martin Schoengauer, whose painting 'The Virgin of the Rose Bush' is in one of the Colmar churches.

So far as the Eastern iconography of the Burning Bush is concerned, at least one Christmas icon must be mentioned; there is a good reproduction of it in an excellent little book called *The Icon* by A. Hackel (Herder, London, 1954). This icon, in bright and beautiful colours, shows the Bush in the form of a circle of twelve burning shrubs. Alongside each one of them is a biblical scene. At the centre, set one beside the other, are the Virgin Mother and the Child. Above all, at the very top of the icon, the Trinity reigns supreme. The scenery consists of rocks, and Mary and her Son are shown reposing in an opening among them. This symbolism echoes certain hymns of the Orthodox Church which on the one hand call Mary (insofar as she is Virgin) 'Rock without cleft', and on the other (insofar as she is Mother) 'Door of Life'. In a broader sense, the purpose of the iconographers, in linking Mary and the Child with the Burning Bush, is to place a symbol of sublime tenderness in the midst of flames representing divine power.

I

THE SHEPHERD

The Lord is my shepherd
Ps. 23.1

During this retreat I want to read you the twenty-third psalm — 'the shepherd's psalm' — and to meditate with you upon it. It is one of the best known psalms; one might even say that to many it is the most beloved of all the psalms. Yet this fact at once raises a question. Why should I return, yet again, to a text you have probably known quite well since you were children, which you yourselves have often reread, and perhaps also heard reinterpreted? Surely there is a risk of my fatiguing you — in a spiritual sense — by insisting on what is already familiar. No! Because I believe that every phrase of Holy Scripture, even after it has been pondered over hundreds of times, still possesses all its essential power. And besides it is eternally new, since each time we receive the Word we are in a new state of soul. When one drinks from a spring the water is always fresh. Let us try then to read the shepherd's psalm together as if we had never heard it before.

There is another reason for choosing this psalm. We live in a world of bustle, speed, war, and ideological conflict; a world of crises and troubles. It is good to draw apart from all this during these three days, and to steep ourselves in the atmosphere of peace, serenity and confidence that belong to this psalm.

With whom are we concerned in the twenty-third psalm? With a sheep and its shepherd. The sheep symbolises a man— a particular man. I think I can say without risk of historical error that the man is King David himself. This psalm is one of those which may with good reason be attributed to David, who was a shepherd himself in his youth, and whose own personal experience is faithfully reflected in it. But the psalm also has a more general application. It is concerned with all

God's sheep, in other words all men and women.

And who is the shepherd in the psalm? David was evidently thinking of the God of Israel, whereas we can think simply of God, the God of all people, the Creator of all men. Nevertheless Christians usually associate the twenty-third psalm with what they have read in Saint John's gospel on the subject of the Good Shepherd. This is in tune with the most ancient traditions of Christian piety, for prior to the third century, when the image of Christ on the Cross became the essential symbol of Christianity, the guise in which the Saviour was represented in Christian art, and in the prayers of the first generations of believers, was that of a young shepherd.

There is no doubt that our Lord, when he spoke of the Good Shepherd, had the twenty-third psalm in mind. He himself had certainly recited it, and had addressed himself to the Father as to the Shepherd whose Son is the Lamb of God. Jesus is at the same time lamb and shepherd; our Shepherd and also the divine Lamb.

I do not want to confuse the words of the twenty-third psalm with those of the fourth Gospel; all I shall do, here and there, is to touch briefly on the parallels between them. When I speak of the shepherd of the twenty-third psalm I shall simply say 'the Shepherd' without any qualification. And I advise you to accept the glorious indeterminateness of this expression, which gives it a broad enough meaning to signify at the same time our Father in heaven, the Son to whom the Father has entrusted his flock, and the Spirit who, within ourselves, leads us — the sheep — towards heavenly pastures.

The twenty-third psalm begins with the verse: 'The Lord is my shepherd; I shall not want'. But in this opening meditation we shall consider only the first part of the verse: 'The Lord is my shepherd'. These words establish a relationship, a juxtaposition; but far more than this they establish an identity between the two subjects in the sentence: on the one hand the Lord, on the other the shepherd. This identity is something of a paradox, for there is an immense contrast between the Lord our God and a shepherd.

The Lord ... No matter whether we consider this term in Hebrew, Greek, Latin or English, it evokes three fundamental ideas. First of all the greatness of the Lord. Then the idea of his power. And lastly the idea of our own utter insignificance in relation to this greatness and power. We are infinitely dependent creatures in the Lord's hands.

A shepherd ... You see the contrast between the very great and the very humble and small. A shepherd is neither powerful nor rich. He is at the service of his employer. He is also at the service of the sheep under his care. The sheep follow him, it is true, but they follow him because he lives for his flock. He has to lead them, feed them, give them shelter, defend them. His whole life is devoted to the sheep — he himself belongs to them. Yet the psalmist declares that *the Lord* is such a man who belongs to his sheep; that the Lord is quite simply a shepherd, a humble shepherd. That is precisely the paradox, the incredible paradox.

Notice here that the psalm does not say 'the shepherd is the Lord.' It does not put forward the idea that the shepherd is raised up to the level of lordship. No, the shepherd does not become Lord. If the first term of the sentence were 'shepherd' and the second 'Lord', the sequence would suggest a kind of magnificent ascension. But on the contrary the word 'Lord' precedes the word 'shepherd'. It is the Lord who is our starting point. Here, as in everything else, the Lord takes the initiative. There is no mounting up from the state of the shepherd to the state of the Lord. There is a descent, a coming down, from the state of Lord to that of shepherd. It is an act of the deepest and most compassionate self-abasement. And this movement of humility and tenderness gives its tone and spirit to the whole of the psalm.

'The Lord is my shepherd.' What we have here is a declaration made with sober decisive authority. It is not a forecast of the future: 'the Lord will be my shepherd.' Nor is it a wish or a prayer: 'Lord, be my shepherd!' It is a simple, tranquil statement of a fact which is already in being: 'The Lord is my shepherd.' This is the true state of things; this is actually so; this is the fact of the matter; this — and not otherwise — is how things really stand. I may turn away from the Shepherd. But such a rejection does not prevent the Lord from remaining thhe Shepherd. He *is* the Shepherd, he is the Shepherd now, he will remain so for ever.

The Lord is not just any kind of shepherd. He is not shepherd in an abstract and general sense. Nor is he the shepherd of his flock as a flock, independently of each one of the sheep that belong to the flock. He is not 'our Shepherd'. Or rather he *is* our Shepherd, but he is also something else and something more. He is *my* Shepherd. The Old Testament prophets spoke clearly of the shepherd of Israel. Yet they did not explain as strongly as the twenty-third psalm the individual and personal side of the relationship between shepherd and sheep. 'My Shepherd' . . . Let us consider rather more closely the implications of the possessive adjective 'my'.

When I say that the Lord is my Shepherd, this means first of all that I belong to the Shepherd. The Shepherd says to me: "Thou art mine; I have an absolute right over thee. Thou art master of neither thy body nor thy soul. Thou art mine.' But to a certain extent this same expression 'my Shepherd' has a double meaning. I can reply to the Shepherd, 'Yes, I am thine, I belong to thee. But, because thou declarest that thou art "my" Shepherd, thou thyself also belongest to me. I also have rights over thee, the rights thou hast given me in allowing me to use the word "my" for thee'. The Shepherd does not turn away from confidence as audacious and demanding as this.

Finally, the expression 'my Shepherd' signifies everything that is unique about the Shepherd's care for me, since he is not Shepherd to me in the same way that he is Shepherd to anyone else. He is each person's Shepherd in a way that is unique and secret. His attitude, his approach, his 'pastoral care' (one can truly call it that) vary according to each individual case. He is 'my Shepherd' not only because he belongs to me as much as I belong to him (as we have seen) but also because he acts as my Shepherd in whatever concerns

66

me, in an exclusive way adapted to me alone, and of which I have — if I dare to put it so — the monopoly.

'The Lord is my shepherd.' We will not go further this evening. But already, in this short affirmation, we have in embryo everything that is developed in the rest of the psalm. Let us lean on this phrase, rest upon it. Whatever may be the shortcomings, the worries, the sorrows that you bring with you to this retreat, as well as the joys and the responses, let a great peace establish itself in your soul. Do not trust in your own feeble strength, but only in the power and grace that flow from the Shepherd, as he carries you on his shoulder or in his arms. Go forward with him, while repeating softly to yourselves: 'The Lord is my Shepherd.'

II

I Shall Not Want

I shall not want
Ps. 23.1

In our first meditation we thought about the fundamental assertion: 'The Lord is my shepherd.' We realised the divine self-abasement, the tenderness, and the intimate bond of belonging to one another that it implies. Now we shall turn to the second part of the first verse of our psalm: 'I shall not want'.

Notice first of all that one cannot isolate these four words from those preceding them. One cannot dissociate or separate 'I shall not want' from 'The Lord is my shepherd', because 'I shall not want' is the direct and immediate consequence of 'The Lord is my shepherd'. It is not as if 'I shall not want' were juxtaposed with the basic affirmation or added to it. The psalm does not say 'The Lord is my shepherd *and* I shall not want'. There is no 'and' here to introduce a new idea. 'Therefore' not 'and' is the word one must take for granted: 'The Lord is my Shepherd, *therefore* I shall not want', or *'because* the Lord is my Shepherd I shall not want.' The Shepherd's care of his flock, the certainty that he will not allow his sheep to lack what they need for their life — all this is contained already in the very essence of the Shepherd's ministry. But notice something more. I drew your attention to the fact that the affirmation 'The Lord is my shepherd' is not a prayer or a wish. It is the declaration of a state, of a situation which exists already. The same applies to the short phrase 'I shall not want.' We do not say 'I hope that my Shepherd will not leave me in want.' Nor do we say, 'O my Shepherd, let me not want'. We affirm calmly that the Shepherd will not abandon us in our distress. We state a fact.

Yet it is just here that comes the difficulty, the paradox, of the text 'I shall not want'. We must not deceive ourselves.

These words are the most difficult of the whole psalm, the hardest to understand, the hardest to accept. For, quite simply, they seem a flagrant contradiction of reality. 'I shall not want'. But if we look around us or read the papers, what do we see, what do we read? Armed conflicts, wars, vast numbers dying of hunger, everywhere the sick. How can we declare that the Shepherd will not allow his own to lack what they need? Many centuries have passed since the psalmist, with astonishing optimism, gave shape to this sentence. But has not the history of those centuries produced cruel and painful denials of his affirmation? Here we touch on the problem of evil. We will not try to resolve it at the moment. But let us remember what the Gospel says. God does not will the hurt of any of his creatures. The present world is not what God willed it to be. The Lord Jesus declared that Satan is the prince of this world.[1] This implies that God has in some manner limited himself; not in his essential all-powerfulness but in the exercise of his supreme power. It is the mystery of the suffering God, suffering with us and for us, in an ineffable way which does not in the least diminish the divine essence but which makes it possible for God to assume voluntarily — not in any sense submit to — a participation in human suffering. The Cross is here and now, beyond space and time. It is forever raised, and it coincides with the victory, the joy, of the Resurrection. At present we shall not dwell on the problem of evil any more than in these general terms. Let us return to the text, which seems so incredible, 'I shall not want'.

The contradiction between this text and the realities of life has been explained in many different ways. Several of these explanations are perfectly justifiable. Some people are in need, but they do not pray to God for help. Others pray, but their prayer lacks faith and fervour. Others pray with faith, but they ask for something which God does not will for them. Others ask for what God wills, but God, for their good, delays

1. John 12.31; 14.30; 16.11.

the granting of their prayer. And then there are those whom God seems to leave in entire distress even when their prayer is genuine and deep; such cases may perhaps be very rare, but they do seem to exist occasionally. What then of 'I shall not want'?

Here again do not let us try to resolve a problem which is beyond us. But let us try to face it in the light of our faith, in the light of divine Love. And in the first place we need more than mere daring. We need the daring to repeat the psalmist's claim without any reservations. Do not let us say 'I shall not want, but . . .' Let us dare to say with entire, absolute confidence: "I shall not want; never . . .' Is this possible? Yes, it is possible if we apply this affirmation to our entire destiny.

Certainly if we confine the saying 'I shall not want' to a particular case and a particular moment, if we isolate this or that episode, if we cut it off from the rest of our lives, we can get the impression that our crying need and our prayer remain without a divine answer. I may be starving, homeless; I may be afflicted, ill. It may seem to me then that I have the right to say 'I am in want'. I can truly say 'I am in need of such and such. I am asking for such and such'; this is a valid meaning for the words 'I am in want' — I need some definite thing. But I have no right to say: 'What I am asking for is lacking'. I have no right, faced with the Shepherd's apparent silence, to conclude that what I need does not exist or is entirely refused to me.

The painful moment when the Shepherd seems to ignore my distress is not my entire life. This moment must be seen in the context of my life as a whole. No, the Shepherd does not ignore my distress, even if he remains silent. But his answer is in a sense diffused throughout the whole course of my existence. He does not give me an answer today. Perhaps it will come tomorrow, perhaps next day, perhaps after a long interval. To perceive the answer I must consider the whole curve of my life, not just some individual point. If I am able to grasp this I shall see that in reality, even if my life appears to consist of long-drawn-out miseries, everything in the past has been grace; everything now is grace. These graces are perhaps very different from what I would have imagined, from what I hoped for, asked for. But never, never, has the Shepherd abandoned me. He has never left me in want.

What? Does it never happen that someone perishes because their most essential needs have been left unfulfilled? Here, more than ever, we must arm ourselves with the audacity of faith. We must dare to answer: 'The moment has come when the divine affirmation is given. The moment of death is the moment of entry into the life of the blessed.' Our faith is so feeble that here we can only realise in a vague and inconsistent way what exactly the cause of our joy should be. Too often we regard eternal life as something like the appendix of a book in which our earthly life is the main text. But no! Just the opposite! Our earthly life is no more than the preface to the book. Eternal life will be the book itself. Our earthly life is like a tunnel. We are in the darkness of the tunnel. But on leaving it we shall enter a landscape of light and beauty. There, on the other side, all our needs — our true needs — will be satisfied for ever, in all superabundance. The curve of our life will then be visible to us in the fullness of its meaning. Then we shall be able to say without hesitation 'I shall not want'.

Unfortunately we are so much infected by present-day materialism that we hardly dare mention eternal life. We fear the taunt of the unbelievers: 'opium of the people'. Always that lack of faith, that lack of the audacity of faith, at the very moment when we ought to take the great leap to the other side. And this is not all. Even in our earthly life, even in the grip of great dangers, great sorrows; if we cling to the Shepherd — if we hold to him with a faith and love that are without reservations — already everything is given. Because all is in Him. If we have Him, his real self, we have all. Even at the very moment when life seems to be about to crush us we shall find — in our act of acceptance, in our renunciation, in our gift of ourselves to the Shepherd — everything we truly need (and we did not know it!) 'O death, where is thy sting?.[1] Suffering may break its bounds like a river in flood. But already a great light will be rising in us and around us, and we shall be repeating: 'The Lord is my shepherd. I shall not want'.

1. I Cor 15.55.

III

The Green Pastures

**He maketh me to lie down in green pastures:
he leadeth me beside the still waters.**

Ps. 23.2

In the last verse we learnt that the Shepherd, precisely because he is the Shepherd, does not abandon his sheep in the midst of their troubles. In spite of the accidents of our earthly life, in spite of events that appear to be victories for suffering and evil, we can be certain — if we consider the whole course of our destiny, both in the beyond as well as here below — that our distress will not be the end for us, and that the Shepherd will provide solutions for all our problems. Because he himself is the solution.

The sheeps' foremost need is nourishment. Their physical life must be sustained. The shepherd in the first place is the one who feeds them, who gives them food and drink. This is the theme which is developed in the second verse of our psalm. And since this psalm is largely symbolic (without ever ceasing to have an immediate application in the physical sense), we must think here of spiritual food and drink as well as of sustenance for our bodies.

'He maketh me to lie down in green pastures'. Let us concentrate first on the expression 'green pastures'. What is a pasture? The idea of a pasture, as far as grazing animals are concerned, implies a certain freedom, a certain limitless abundance. The sheep that belong to the shepherd do not get rations from him, or shares that are strictly measured out. They come and go as they please within the bounds of the pasture, and feed on the grass as long as they want, until they are satisfied. In the same way (on the spiritual plane) our Shepherd does not weigh out the nourishment he gives us day by day. He treats us liberally, indeed generously. Among the thoughts he sends us, the words he lets us hear, the opportunities he offers us (and our pasture consists of all these things), he leaves us free to choose those which respond best to our own taste and our present needs.

Green pastures ... As a matter of fact there have never been many green pastures in Palestine. Except in certain parts of Galilee, Palestine lacks both greenness and pastures. It is a hard, dry country, full of stones and rocks. There is nothing resembling the prairies of the west. The psalmist, when he speaks of green pastures, expresses a kind of nostalgia for an ideal landscape. But at the same time he is making an act of faith. He is declaring that the Shepherd can, in a flash, create green pastures for his sheep, by transforming what was formerly arid and sterile into fertile fields .

This transforming power operates in our own lives. Sometimes, perhaps often, our circumstances on earth and the setting of our interior lives give the impression of a barren stretch of desert. But then, all at one, if my heart turns towards the Shepherd, everything changes in a moment. A vista of great possibilities opens up for me. The desert becomes green. It begins to shoot. It becomes a pasture.

This prairie where we can now graze is a 'green' pasture. What does this adjective mean here? What is the significance of the colour green? The pasture is green because the grass that the Shepherd offers us is young and tender. Old grass which is decaying is stiff and discoloured. But when we see the green grass we know that it will remain fresh for a long time. Surrounded by green grass, the sheep can graze without fear of finding themselves short, without any anxiety for the morrow.

Green is the colour of Spring, the symbol of hope. It heralds a renewal. He who trusts himself to the Shepherd leads, so to speak, a 'green' life. His interior landscape is one full of fresh hope. He goes forward in an eternal springtime. He does not become old as his years increase, because each day he is growing, each day he is renewed, each day he sees and hears and accomplishes things which once he would not have dared to dream of. And this is because he has entrusted his life to the Shepherd. The only way of staying young is to live close to the Shepherd, for him, in him.

'To lie down in green pastures'. Do you see how strong the expression is? The sheep are so much 'at home' in the Shepherd's pastures that they can relax completely, they can lie down with a field of entire security and confidence. They can rest. They can sleep. They know that the Shepherd will defend them against all attacks. In the green pastures that belong to the Shepherd the sheep find perfect peace. 'To lie down in green pastures'. Surely this is what we need. To escape from a feverish life, to forget our worries, to relax, to stretch ourselves out near the Shepherd, under his protection. And this is, in fact, what is offered us. 'Come unto me . . . I will give you rest . . . and ye shall find rest unto your souls'[1].

'He maketh me to lie down'. It is not as though we ourselves, being tired, were asking the Shepherd for permission to lie down. The Shepherd takes the initiative. He does not force us to lie down in green pastures, but he arranges everything in such a way that we are able to lie down very close to him. He invites us to do so. And this is not merely so that we may recover from exhaustion. It is when we are in a position of abandon and trusting tenderness that the Shepherd wants to communicate with us. Remember how a Master and his disciples lay at ease around the table of a paschal meal, one evening in Jerusalem, in an upper chamber . . .

'He leadeth me beside the still waters'. Food alone is not enough. The body must also be refreshed. One's bodily thirst must be quenched; likewise the thirst of one's soul. And it is not for us to discover what will appease our thirst. It is for the Shepherd to lead his sheep towards the refreshing waters.

At the moment we shall not pursue all the meanings of 'he leadeth'. We will return to this later, in the context of another verse. Let us only note, in passing, the deeply personal relationship between the Shepherd and his sheep. The psalmist

1. Matt. 11. 28-29.

does not say: 'He maketh *us* to lie down . . . He leadeth *us*', but 'He maketh *me* to lie down . . . He leadeth *me.*'

Where is the Shepherd leading me? 'Beside the still waters'. The water here has two meanings, and both are at the same time material and spiritual. First, water refreshes. To an organism which is parched and arid it brings relief; it quells the torment of thirst, it gives new energy and life to the tissues. Water also purifies. It washes, removes stains. It removes every trace of dirt. Thus it satisfies two fundamental needs of our existence, refreshment and cleansing. The desire for water is stronger, even more intense, than the desire for food. 'As pants the heart for cooling streams . . .'[1]

The Shepherd does not lead his sheep towards just any kind of water. The psalmist speaks of 'still waters'. Why 'still'? Sheep have a great dislike for any water that is agitated or turbulent; they will not drink from torrents, waterfalls or fast-running rivers. They need calm waters, those which are more or less still and unruffled (this is why shepherds often prefer to draw some water and give it to the sheep in suitable vessels). Here there is a profound symbolism. If a sheep is not able to drink quietly, then the water in question has not been given to it by the shepherd, and the animal is wilfully following a useless caprice. The water which the Shepherd gives is never disturbed. It is offered, given without stint, and absorbed slowly, gently. I cannot draw near to the water provided by the Shepherd unless my soul is first of all at peace.

One more point, on which we shall conclude this meditation. 'He leadeth me beside the still waters'. Let us examine one of the words more closely: 'besides'. Geometrically speaking, this means that when we want to drink we do not go towards the water by means of a perpendicular line. We follow steadily along a line which is more or less parallel to the watercourse. We walk quite close to the water all the time, following along its bank. And thus we can drink whenever we

1. Ps. 42. 1, as translated in a well-known English hymn.

want to. We do not need to diverge from our path to go towards the water, because the water and we ourselves follow the same route. The water is always close to us, at our side. It is always within reach, to the same extent that we always remain close to the Shepherd. Because, if we want to plumb the depths of spiritual reality, we shall see that the Shepherd and the water — the Living Water — are not two separate entities. The Shepherd himself is the Water. 'If any man thirst, let him come unto me, and drink'[1]

1. John 7.37.

IV

The Restorer

He restoreth my soul: he leadeth me in the paths of righteousness for his name's sake.

Ps. 23.3

We have already been able to stay ourselves, to rest in confidence, upon several affirmations full of promise and hope. I know that the Shepherd is *my* Shepherd — my own Shepherd. I know that in the last extremity he will never allow me to lack what is needful. I know that he reveals the green pastures where I shall feed. I know that beside me — which means where he himself is — I shall always find living water, the still water that will quench my thirst.

Up till now we have been thinking about what the Shepherd does to take care of me, to maintain my life, both in the physical and spiritual sense, and to provide for the most basic needs of my existence. Now, with the third verse of the psalm, we go on to an order of ideas, or rather of realities, that is both greater and deeper. For here the Shepherd does not only concern himself with enabling things to continue as they are. He is going to remake past events, to bring back to life that which has been destroyed or atrophied by misfortune or accident. This third verse is like a window opening onto a new landscape. Through it a breath of fresh air, a different atmosphere, reaches our souls. We are going to discover the Shepherd as the one who brings healing wherever there is sickness and death. We are going to recognise him as our Saviour and Redeemer.

'He restoreth my soul'. First of all the expression 'my soul' needs clarifying. The Hebrew word *nephesh*, which the psalmist uses here, has a stronger and much more complex meaning than the English word 'soul', for it links together the ideas of spirit, of breath and breathing, and of vital essence and personality. It also has a certain link with the idea of blood. 'He restoreth my life' would be a better rendering here. And what is it that the Shepherd does for this life of mine? He restores it. The verb 'restore' is very rich in meaning. A house is restored when it is put into good condition again. A king is restored when he is re-established on his throne. The human body is restored when it is invigorated by food or rest. To restore is to make whole. And restoration only takes place in circumstances where there has been some loss or injury. The consequences of loss or damage must be wiped out — as when the mending of a tear obliterates it. But here there is more besides; some sort of amends must be made for the wrong. There must be a counterbalancing of evil by good.

Let us see how this applies to our personal life. To say that the Shepherd restores our life means very much more than that he strengthens his sheep by providing food and drink. It also means far more than that the Shepherd can merely cure us when we are physically ill. The Shepherd brings about the essential restoring of my life when he comes 'to seek and to save that which was lost'[1].

That which was lost . . . The lost sheep . . . Later on, in the Gospel, we have a moving description of the sheep that has deserted its shepherd — this desertion is, in fact, the loss — and of the Good Shepherd who leaves his flock to seek for, and find, the lost sheep — this is, in fact, salvation. 'He restoreth my soul: ' at times when it seems that I am hopelessly overwhelmed by sin, when I feel I have lost all the goodness I ever possessed, the redeeming power of the Shepherd will tear me away from sin and evil. I deliberately say redeeming power. Because the Shepherd buys me back. He only gives salvation in giving himself — his whole self.

But we shall not linger here over the idea of the Shepherd as Redeemer. For it belongs rather to the Gospel. If we return to our psalm, however, we shall see the meaning of loss and salvation, of wounds and healing, through the eyes of the psalmist himself.

1. Luke 19.10.

'He leadeth me in the paths of righteousness'. This sentence explains two things. On the one hand it shows the origin and essence of all our spiritual ills. When we talk of the sickness or death of a soul we mean the condition of a sheep that will not let itself be led by the Shepherd along the right path. And on the other hand the phrase indicates what the restoring of a soul consists of: the sheep is 'restored' when it accepts the Shepherd as guide and follows him wherever he leads.

'He leadeth me'. The Shepherd does not go alongside his sheep. He does not walk behind the flock. He goes ahead. He is the leader of his sheep and their guide. And here there is a difference between eastern and western practice. The shepherds in our western countries often walk at the rear; they are concerned with ensuring that their sheep stay together, that none are left behind; they urge them on vocally and the sheep go forward along paths that are smooth and well defined. In the east there are seldom any well-marked paths. The shepherd has to go ahead of his flock to show the way as well as to defend the flock against possible attacks by wild animals. In short the shepherd has a double function. He opens up the path and he takes the responsibility. He guides and directs. And these are precisely the two tasks of our Shepherd as leader.

The function of the sheep is to follow the shepherd. To follow: this word recurs so often in the Gospel ('Follow thou me!' ... 'They followed him'). What does 'to follow' really mean? It means to come after someone, to come closely behind him. It means to go in the same direction as him without wandering to left or right, without breaking away, without running on ahead, and without wanting to go more slowly or more quickly than the leader. It means to persevere in accompanying him. It means to make a point of rejoining him if separated. But you cannot constantly follow someone unless a certain emotional relationship exists. You become attached to the one you follow, you abandon yourself to him. There is even an interior and mental way of following a person. If somebody says 'Do you follow me?' he means 'Do you grasp the meaning of my words, do you thoroughly understand what I mean?' How much there is in the word 'follow'! How much is implied by the relationship between the Shepherd who guides and the sheep that follow him.

'He leadeth me'. Where is the Shepherd leading his sheep? 'In the paths of righteousness'. The word 'righteousness' is a complicated one. There are few adjectives in Hebrew. Nouns are often used in their place, and this gives a heavier and more solemn tone to a sentence. 'Paths of righteousness' means 'the right paths'. But 'right' can have two meanings here. The right paths may perhaps be the shortest ones, those which are best adapted, most suitable for attaining the ends which the Shepherd has in mind. They are the paths that can be followed safely, without fear of going astray. The right paths are also perhaps the righteous paths, the ways of justice and goodness. These two ideas apply to all the 'leads' we receive from the Shepherd. To live our lives under his guidance means that we do not restrict these 'leads' to a few great occasions or decisions, to a few choices of supreme moral importance. We can be guided by the Shepherd all day long — whenever, for instance, we decide to go out, to write a letter, to visit someone, to discuss something, and so on. To the Shepherd and the sheep there are no such things as small decisions. Nothing is small that corresponds to an intention of the Shepherd's. But only through quiet, prayer, and inner dialogue with our Shepherd can we enter into the guided life. 'He leadeth me' — me, in the deepest of personal relationships.

'For his name's sake.' These words may seem difficult to understand. The Shepherd certainly does not desire that his attitude towards the flock should win prestige and praise for himself. He does not seek glory for his own name. But he does want to implement to the full all that is meant by the name 'shepherd'. Being the Shepherd, he wants to be the Good Shepherd, the true Shepherd. And he also wants to show himself faithful. In a sense he has put his name, his signature, to a 'contract' which links him with his sheep. He cannot, nor does he wish to, disavow or dishonour this name and this invisible signature. Let us note that the Shepherd himself is tied by this 'covenant'. He took the initiative. How often we do violence to this relationship which we ourselves did nothing to originate. But he — 'for his name's sake' — will be eternally faithful to this 'covenanted grace'. In offering it to us at every moment, in spite of our faults, he reveals himself as the Restorer. 'He restoreth my soul'.

V.

For Thou art with Me

**Yea, though I walk through the valley of the
shadow of death, I will fear no evil: for thou
art with me; thy rod and thy staff they
comfort me.**
Ps. 23.4

This fourth verse of the shepherd's psalm is the centre-
point of the whole psalm. It is the key verse. It marks a
turning point. And in a moment I will tell you why.

But first as a preliminary I want to show you how the
thoughts in this verse are developed, and also how strong the
construction is. The theme here is no longer the shepherd as
giver of food and guidance to his sheep. We are now thinking
of him as the defender of his flock. This theme is worked out
under the form of three ideas, or rather of two metaphors
with an idea inserted between them. The first metaphor shows
the dangers that threaten the sheep. Then comes a declaration
of heartfelt trust; all fear is banished, and the reason for this
victory over fear is explained in two or three words. Finally
symbolism is again introduced so as to confirm, to crystallize,
the act of faith and confidence by means of familiar imagery.

'Yea, though I walk through the valley of the shadow of
death . . .' Here the danger is described by a comparison borrowed from true life in Palestine. The flock or the traveller
may enter a *wadi* — this is an Arab word which means a deep
gorge between towering cliffs, where daylight hardly pene-
trates. A jackal, a fox, a wolf, a robber, may be waiting there
in ambush, ready to attack any men or sheep who come near.
The danger is great. The Hebrew words used by the psalmist
suggest something far more sinister than just a valley which
narrows and becomes rather shadowy and dim. They convey
the idea of shadows which are profoundly dark. The Hebrew
expression *tsalmareth* means the shadow of death itself, the

night which reigns in *sheol*, the place of the dead. The sheep that belong to the Shepherd are exposed to many risks; to enemy attack, illness, death. And beyond the physical risks we are endangered by temptation, as well as by spiritual sickness and death.

Are we going to be frightened? Are we going to shrink back in anxiety, perhaps terror, before such dangers? There are two magnificent Old Testament texts which exhort us not to be afraid. The prophet Amos says: 'Seek him that... turneth the shadow of death into the morning'[1]. And Isaiah: 'The people that walked in darkness have seen a great light: they that dwell in the land of the shadow of death, upon them hath the light shined'.[2] In the Gospel too these same words were later to be put on the lips of Zacariah[3].

At the present day, more than at any other time in history, the sheep that belong to the Shepherd seem to be exposed to the shadows of fear, solitude, frustration, despair, lack of faith. And nevertheless, whether in the case of one who weeps alone in his solitary room, or of another who is threatened by cancer and is about to be laid on the operating table, the Shepherd is there close at hand. He himself goes ahead, in front of his flock of sheep, in front of each individual sheep which belongs to him. He will surely do battle for them. Even if he allows the 'shadow of death' to rest for a moment on one of his flock, it is only to enable this same sheep to enter into a new era of light — into full daylight.

And now, after picturing the danger — 'though I walk through the valley of the shadow of death' — comes the calm affirmation 'I will fear no evil'. At the start of the psalm the faithful sheep asserted 'I shall not want'. But besides being set free from need, all the sheep are set free from fear. 'For thou art with me'. Here we have the reason that justifies our freedom from fear. Whatever may happen to us our confi-

1. Amos 5.8
2. Isaiah 9.2.
3. Luke 1.79.

dence is unshaken because the Shepherd is with us, with *me*.

'With me . . .' There are two ways of being 'with' another person. You can be in the same place as someone, close to him, or indeed face to face with him. And yet despite this physical proximity you and he can remain entire strangers, mentally in isolation from one another. On the other hand you can be 'with' another person in the sense of being at one with him, having things in common, of entering into a vital interchange of ideas. Then there is no longer merely a physical closeness but an existential sharing. The Greek language shows a clear appreciation of this difference, for separate prepositions are used to distinguish the two meanings: in the first case *sun*, in the second *meta*. Thus the Greek translation of our verse renders its meaning with perfect accuracy by using the preposition *meta*: 'Thou art with me', *met'emou*, means 'thou enterest into my life'.

I have already told you that the fourth verse of the shepherd's psalm is its central point. It unites the psalm. At the same time it cuts it in half. Have you noticed that up until now the psalmist speaks of the Shepherd in the third person singular — 'he'? But from the fourth verse onwards he will be speaking *to* the Shepherd (not any longer *of* him) and will be using the second person singular, the pronoun *thou*.

Luther said somewhere that religion is largely a matter of pronouns. You probably know the theory of the Jewish philosopher Martin Buber on 'I and Thou'. So long as we speak of others in terms of 'he' 'she' or 'they' we are really thinking of them as 'it', as beings of a neuter kind. It is only when we think of them in terms of 'thou' (how much stronger it is than 'you') that we enter into a truly living and personal relationship.

But now let us leave the linguistic approach. What matters is to see how much, from this verse onwards, the whole tone of the psalm changes. Before it, admittedly, we had some great and splendid affirmations of faith. They *concerned* the Shepherd. Now we are addressing ourselves directly *to him*. We are speaking to him. And we are letting ourselves speak from the heart. Furthermore we are no longer concerned with confidence but with affection and tenderness. This is the moment when love itself bursts out into our psalm. It has never been lacking, but with this fourth verse — 'for *thou art with me*' — it reveals itself openly as love, like fire blazing out from a volcano.

'Thy rod and thy staff they comfort me'. These last words of the verse develop the affirmation of the divine Presence. And to give impact to their meaning a new comparison, borrowed from the life of a shepherd, is used to show how this Presence manifests itself. 'Thy rod and thy staff...' These two terms are not synonymous. Each of the objects in question was used by the Hebrew shepherds and each has a profound significance. 'Thy rod...' in Hebrew *shebet*. The *shebet* was a shortish wooden club, strengthened at one end with metal. It was used as a defensive weapon, to protect the flock from dangerous animals.

'Thy staff...' In Hebrew *mishenet*. The word conveys the idea of support. The shepherd himself sometimes leant on this longish staff of his. He also used it to guide and help his sheep. The top of the *mishenet* was curved over in the shape of a crook. By means of this crook the shepherd could if necessary catch hold of a sheep by the neck or leg. And a light touch of it could serve to direct the animal to left or right. The *mishenet* was also used to assist a sheep when it was crossing a stream.

The shepherd's staff seems to be the origin of the royal sceptre. As a matter of fact, sceptres first appeared in Egypt at the time of a dynasty of shepherd-kings, the Hyksos. Our Shepherd too is a King, our King. He does not wish to have any other sceptre than the staff which symbolises his pastoral care.

'They comfort me'. For us the rod and the staff are not instruments of intimidation. They signify that our Shepherd is our defender and helper. They inspire us with assurance and confidence. 'Thou are with me...' Beloved Shepherd, what could we do without thee?

VI

The Table Laid

**Thou preparest a table before me in the presence of
mine enemies: thou anointest my head with oil;
my cup runneth over.**
Ps. 23.5

The last verse—evoking as it did the shadow of death, the
sweet presence of the Shepherd, and also his rod and his staff
— was in a sense unique both by reason of its deep feeling
and by its blend of violence and tenderness. When we turn
now to the fifth verse of our psalm, does it not seem that we
are descending, as a musician would say, into a lower key?
Are we not returning to the green pastures and refreshing
waters of the second verse? Surely to ponder once again upon
the subject of feeding is to go back to the psalm's original
level? Are we not letting ourselves slide into a state of mere
peace and quiet, after having undergone the experience of the
great shadow and of salvation?

This is no more than a deceptive impression. It is true that
in this fifth verse the psalmist resumes the theme of food and
drink which already occurred in the second. But he is going
to give it an entirely new strength by raising it, amplifying it.
Once again in the language of music, I would say that from a
delicate cantabile he is going to make a fortissimo.

'Thou preparest a table before me in the presence of mine
enemies'. These last words 'in the presence of mine enemies'
show how completely different the present situation is from
the picture of grazing sheep in the second verse. Our enemies:
we have seen what kind of enemies they are, the evil powers
that lie in wait for us in the valley of the shadow of death.
There is a physical hurt and there is also moral evil. This table
that the Shepherd prepares for us is a challenge to danger, sin,
and death. The enemies have not vanished. They are watching
us, they will threaten us until our last moments. Nevertheless

the Shepherd invites us to his table under their very eyes. This is what is so moving about the verse. On the one hand the power of the shadows that threaten the sheep. On the other the power of the Shepherd, who feeds his trusting flock. Above our heads, the Shepherd and our Enemy confront one another. 'In the presence of mine enemies' — Yes! But the Shepherd has prepared the table for each one of us. He has placed it 'before me' in such a way that what I see before me is the table and not the enemy. My attention is not drawn towards the wolves that prowl around. It is concentrated on the Shepherd and his gifts.

'Thou preparest a table'. Obviously we should not think here of the banquets that are described in the Gospel. In fact there is not really a table here at all. One should imagine rather the five thousand whom Jesus told to sit down on the grass so that he might multiply the loaves for them. The Shepherd prepares a table in the sense that he has chosen a quiet, sheltered situation, a grassy place where there are no vipers as snakes or scorpions. And furthermore the word 'table' introduces the idea of hospitality and good cheer. The table represents a meal that is shared. The banquet of the Messiah is a symbol of the Kingdom of God.

The table which the Shepherd prepares also has another significance that is obviously far deeper than the meaning of our psalm. This meaning is conveyed in the words of the Gospel: 'I am the living bread which came down from heaven: if any man eat of this bread, he shall live for ever'[1]. It is also implicit in the words of the Book of Revelation: 'If any man hear my voice, and open the door, I will come in to him, and will sup with him, and he with me'[2]. I shall not dwell on these texts which are already familiar to you. But I would like to quote one which perhaps you do not know. It is a short passage from the Koran entitled 'The Table'. Listen to this: 'The Apostles said "O Jesus son of Mary, is thy Lord able to send down to us a table from heaven? ... We

1. John 6.51.
2. Rev. 3.20.

desire to eat of it and to make our hearts to be at rest". Jesus, son of Mary, said "O God our Lord, send down to us a table from heaven, that shall be a feast for the first and the last of us and a sign from Thee. And provide for us, for Thou art the best of providers". God said, "Verily I do send that table down to you, but whichsoever of you hereafter disbelieves, I shall chastise him as no other being has been chastised".' These words were not written by a Christian, but what Christian could fail to respond to the intuition and emotion in which they are steeped?

'Thou anointest my head with oil'. Among the Hebrews oil was precious; it stood for material prosperity, peace, sweetness. Kings and priests were anointed with oil. Either oil or perfume was poured onto the heads of guests. Therefore it is natural that the Shepherd should use oil to anoint the sheep for whom he has prepared a table. Finally the word 'Messiah' itself means 'The Anointed One'. But I think that the psalmist wanted to allude here to something rather different, to an everyday and very homely scene. When in the evening the sheep are brought back to the fold they pass one by one before their shepherd, who examines them to see whether any of them have received some hurt. Perhaps one of them is limping. The heads of many have been scratched with thorns. It is then that the Shepherd pours into our wounds — our faults, our anxieties — the most sweet oil of his compassion and tenderness.

'My cup runneth over'. The Shepherd quenches the thirst of his sheep. But if we compare these words 'My cup runneth over' with the words of the second verse 'He leadeth me beside the still waters' we can see the difference at once. In the first instance we were concerned with water that was untroubled. Now we are thinking of water that overflows. In the first case it was a stream of water to which the sheep themselves drew near; they did not receive the water from the Shepherd's hand. Now the Shepherd has drawn water in a vessel and himself offers it to them. The Shepherd's attitude is loving and giving.

89

'My cup . . .' The word 'cup' has two different meanings in Holy Scripture. Sometimes it is a cup of bitterness and testing, like the cup which Our Lord, in the garden, prayed that his Father might take away from him, and like the cup of which he said to his disciples: 'Are ye able to drink of the cup that I shall drink of?'[1] But sometimes the cup is a symbol of blessing and joy. It is in this sense that the psalmist says: 'I will take the cup of salvation, and call upon the name of the Lord'[2]. The cup that our Shepherd holds out to us is the cup of salvation.

This cup, my cup, 'runneth over'. The Shepherd is generous. He does not limit the water to the size of the cup. He fills it right up to the brim and even beyond. The water overflows the cup. Grace is given abundantly, super-abundantly. But even so, will not the water in the cup be exhausted very soon? Is not the cup going to be emptied? The best way to make sure that it is always overflowing is to place it under a running spring; then the water will overflow the cup, which will never be empty. I shall never lack water or suffer dryness or thirst if I dwell always close to the source, close to the Living Water, to the Person who himself is both water and spring. We have already said this in meditating on the second verse of the psalm. The further truth that our fifth verse brings to us, in relation to the water, is the idea of super-abundance, of divine lavishness. With it is the idea that the interior life of a sheep, when given without reservation to the Shepherd, is a fountain that is constantly overflowing. Love supreme is limitless love, love beyond all bounds — 'mad love' in the eyes of men.

1. Matt. 20.22.
2. Ps. 116.13.

VII

For Ever

Surely goodness and mercy shall follow me all the days of my life: and I will dwell in the house of the Lord for ever.
Ps. 23.6

Now we have come to the last verse of the shepherd's psalm, and to the final meditation of our retreat. For a moment let us look back over the spiritual journey we have made together: the fundamental affirmation that the Lord is 'my Shepherd', the act of confidence which makes us say that we shall lack nothing, the picture of green pastures and still waters, the salvation that is brought to the wounded soul, the following after the divine Guide, the light which awaits us beyond the valley of shadows, the cry of faith 'Thou art with me', the joyful acceptance of the Master's rod and staff, the table that is prepared for the sheep, the anointing with the oil of sweetness, and the cup that is filled to overflowing.

What is the end of this poem to be? What is its final affirmation? It is to be an expansion to infinity of what has already been said. The psalmist does not want to leave us with the impression that although these things 'happen' they are no more than episodes, fleeting incidents, exceptional graces. In this sixth and last verse he reveals distant horizons instead of near ones, and also the perspectives of eternity — those things which will be 'for ever'.

The verse begins with the adverb 'surely'. There are two different ways in which this word can be used. It can add emphasis at the end of a sentence, where it means 'truly' or 'indeed,' where it says 'Yes, things are indeed just as I have told you: I have explained the precise truth'. Alternatively the affirmation may be placed at the start of the sentence (as in the Gospel phrase, 'Verily, Verily, I say unto you'). In such cases, where the sentence begins with 'surely' or 'truly', the speaker seems to say to his hearer 'Listen carefully. Pay attention to what I am going to say because it is the truth'. In the present instance the psalmist has used the word in this second way. He is not concentrating on the actual content of what he is going to say but on its authenticity, on the absolute truth of the message. It is the attitude of faith, which speaks primarily from a profound personal conviction. Then afterwards he goes on to explain the message itself.

What then is the final message of the shepherd's psalm? Let us divide the verse into two parts. The first relates to a soul — a sheep — which is in a state of pilgrimage. The second declares the state of the soul that has finally arrived, the state of the sheep which will dwell for ever in the presence of the Shepherd.

'Goodness and mercy shall follow me all the days of my life'. Goodness and mercy are two attributes of the Shepherd. These two qualities are not mentioned here by chance. They are essentially complementary to one another. Goodness: this means the good but it also means bountifulness. It is the good which we ought to do, and also the goodness we ought to receive. The Shepherd represents both good and goodness to a supreme degree. Moses asked God, 'Shew me thy glory'. But God replied to him, 'I will make all my goodness pass before thee'[1]. Mercy: this means pity, compassion, pardon. Goodness and mercy cannot be separated. In our weakness we are always violating the ideal of goodness. Thus it is needful that divine Mercy should intervene to grant us the forgiveness we cannot give ourselves. Another psalm reiterates this: 'Have mercy upon me, O God, according to thy loving kindness: according unto the multitude of thy tender mercies blot out my transgressions'[2].

'Goodness and mercy shall follow me . . .' Does it not seem a little strange that goodness and mercy should follow after us? Would it not be more appropriate for them to go on ahead, and for us to follow after them? Let us remember that

1. Exodus 33, 18-19.
2. Ps. 51.1.

the psalmist is speaking of a flock of sheep. It is for the Shepherd to lead the way in front of his flock. Goodness and mercy accompany us from the rear. They are attributes of the Shepherd, but they are less than he. Thus they may aptly be compared to the sheep-dogs that run along behind a flock and round up any sheep which are lagging. Or rather they are like the 'Hound of Heaven' of which the poet Francis Thompson speaks. He does not bark, he does not bite, but one can never escape his loving, poignant pursuit.

> 'Night and nigh draws the chase
> With unperturbed pace . . .'

Nevertheless it is only an abstraction to discriminate between the attributes of a person. In reality the Shepherd himself, the Incarnation of goodness and mercy, is behind us as well as ahead. We intuitively picture him as in front of us, since he is our model. But at the times when his image seems to grow dim, his own action of goodness and mercy assails us from the rear — from behind us — and it is in vain that we try to flee 'down the arches of the years . . . down the labyrinthine ways of my own mind; and. in the mist of tears . . . and under running laughter . . . from those strong Feet that followed, followed after'.
And thus the moment when

> 'Halts by me that footfall:
> Is my gloom, after all,
> Shade of His hand, outstretched caressingly?
> "Ah, fondest, blindest, weakest,
> I am He whom thou seekest!
> Thou dravest love from thee, who dravest Me"[1].

'Goodness and mercy shall follow me all the days of my life'. This is what the last verse of the twenty-third psalm

1. Francis Thompson: *The Hound of Heaven*.

wishes, so to speak, to impress on our souls. 'All the days of my life'. The great experiences that have been described, the great affection that exists between the Shepherd and his sheep, are not matters of a single hour, a single day, a single year. They are destined to endure. And even death itself when we meet it, in a little while, will not interrupt them. 'All the days of my life' . . . this means our earthly pilgrimage, the journeyings of the sheep as they follow the Shepherd. But at the end of this pilgrimage an even better state is offered to us.

'And I shall dwell in the house of the Lord for ever'. Here we are no longer concerned with 'the days of my life', but with what will come to pass 'for ever', even after my life is ended. Here we turn to my eternal life with the Shepherd. 'I shall dwell in the house of the Lord'. We know that David, who was almost certainly the author of this psalm, longed passionately to build a temple for the Lord. The prophet Nathan told him that this was not the will of God: 'Thus saith the Lord, Shalt thou build me an house for me to dwell in?'[1] Men have always tended to enclose their God within a visible structure. God wants first of all to make his dwelling-place in our souls. 'Behold, I stand at the door and knock . . .'[2]. If I open the door to him, and let him come into my soul, my own house becomes the house of God — not the temple, the sanctuary, the tabernacle, but the house — with all that this word 'house' implies of the simple, the familiar, the everyday. 'I shall dwell . . .' I shall not be, in this house of my soul which has become the house of God, an occasional visitor, a transient. Nor shall I be received ceremoniously in a drawing room or in the fine front rooms, but I shall be the permanent resident, I shall live and move about freely in this house. I shall have my kitchen there, and my bedroom. It is my daily life which will run its course in the intimacy of God's presence. He will live in my heart — and I in his.

1. Rev. 3.20.
2. Sam. 7.5.

'For ever . . .' These are the last two words of our psalm. No longer do we say only 'all the days of my life,' but 'for ever'. In one of our first meditations I told you what a mistake it is to think of eternal life as a vague continuation of our earthly life. This earthly life, I repeat, is nothing more than a preface. That to which God calls us is eternal light and eternal joy. Everything which — so it seems — God has withheld from me in this world, along with all the other and even greater treasures which he has stored up for the day of my coming home — I shall find them all when he welcomes me in his arms. The supreme joy will be the limitless intimacy with the Shepherd. Each one of his sheep, no longer merely following after him or resting at his feet, will be carried on his shoulders, held against his breast. In the Shepherd's love will be discovered the Alpha and the Omega, the essence of reality, the cause and purpose of all creation — the total love, the absolute love, the limitless love which moves both the souls of men and the stars of heaven.

We have finished our meditation on the shepherd's psalm. Alas, it has been so short and so superficial! May this poem, this song, continue to echo in our souls! May we find light and joy and strength in repeating a few of its inspired words: 'The Lord is my shepherd, I shall not want . . . Though I walk through the valley of the shadow of death, I will fear no evil . . . Thou art with me'.